sadie frost
crazy days

my autobiography

sadie frost
crazy days
my autobiography

JOHN BLAKE

Published by John Blake Publishing Ltd,
3 Bramber Court, 2 Bramber Road,
London W14 9PB, England

www.johnblakepublishing.co.uk

www.facebook.com/Johnblakepub facebook

twitter.com/johnblakepub twitter

First published in hardback in 2010

This edition published in paperback in 2012

ISBN: 978 1 84358 371 4

All rights reserved. No part of this publication may be reproduced, stored in a retrieval system, or in any form or by any means, without the prior permission in writing of the publisher, nor be otherwise circulated in any form of binding or cover other than that in which it is published and without a similar condition including this condition being imposed on the subsequent publisher.

British Library Cataloguing-in-Publication Data:

A catalogue record for this book is available from the British Library.

Design by www.envydesign.co.uk

Printed and bound in Great Britain by CPI Group (UK) Ltd

1 3 5 7 9 10 8 6 4 2

© Text copyright Sadie Frost 2012

Papers used by John Blake Publishing are natural, recyclable products made from wood grown in sustainable forests. The manufacturing processes conform to the environmental regulations of the country of origin.

Every attempt has been made to contact the relevant copyright-holders, but some were unobtainable. We would be grateful if the appropriate people could contact us.

Dedication
To Mum and Dad
Tom and Betty
'Now it all makes sense'

Acknowledgements

I would like to thank my four beautiful children, Fin, Raff, Iris and Rudy.
My brothers and sisters: Tim, Dan, Simon, Jamie, Toby, Sunshine, Jessie, Holly and Jade.
Frosty, Anne Vaughan, Robert Davidson, Gary, Jude, Ania, Mina, Chip and Heidi, Francis Ridley, Daniel Bee, Laura Reid, Simon Benham and Zoe Lewis.

Contents

Chapter One	Mary and David	1
Chapter Two	Sadie Vaughan	33
Chapter Three	Growing Up	69
Chapter Four	That Boy	103
Chapter Five	Finding My Feet	135
Chapter Six	Love and Marriage	165
Chapter Seven	Big Changes	193
Chapter Eight	Coming Home	231

Primrose Hill

I smell paint. Big hands scoop me up – from my cradle. I'm suspended through air. Wrapped in a blanket. Cold air touches my throat. I jolt. Through every step. Big feet. Left, right, left, right. Walking up. Up. Up a long path, a hill, dark green and dewy. Streetlamps flick past. Up, further up the hill, to the top. I'm lifted in the air, up high into darkness.

I see buildings, lights. The birdcage. I twist my head to look up. Stars – all the night's stars for me to see.

CHAPTER ONE

Mary and David

Mary

With a finger, Mary wiped the bead of sweat from her forehead, tracing its journey down her temple. It was a useless task as no sooner had she brushed it away than more beads formed on her chest, her neck and even her arms. It was as if what was inside of her was pushing everything outwards. She repeated the words to herself, 'If the contractions are two minutes apart you are entering the final stage of labo – ' She resisted the urge to shout out and forced herself to concentrate on the facts in the book, dog-eared and dirty, clutched to her chest like a bible. The childbirth manual that she'd found in a second-hand bookshop in Camden Town was her only source of knowledge. There was no one else she had been able to ask about her expanding stomach and all the complicated feelings that came with it.

After the cramping pain had subsided she tipped her

head back and studied the anaemic little delivery room that they had shoved her into at the Whittington Hospital. The only sound, apart from her own breathing, was the ticking of the clock on the wall, which displayed the date in a little box within the face: 19 June 1965. So this was to be the day. She gripped the book to her breast and nursed her belly with the other hand, rubbing the material of the crème anglaise-coloured nightdress that she'd chosen with great care for the birth. She'd so desperately wanted the birth of her first baby to be special, but she was totally alone. No mother or father or sisters or friends. She'd resigned herself to that months ago. *But I want him to be here. Him. Where is he?* Where was he when she needed him? Even the nurses were too busy to sit and comfort her, and she felt ashamed. Of what, she didn't know exactly.

She returned to the book and wondered if she would ever have got this far without it. All her friends back home were busy with homework or enjoying school discos. London was huge and unfriendly, and however much she adored him, *he* hadn't been much help at all. A vast, shuddering pain interrupted her reading and the book slipped from her grasp as she reacted to the searing rip – as if someone was chopping her open from the inside. Her cry brought a nurse to the door, a stern woman with a time-worn face.

'Nurse!' said Mary, panting. 'I think my baby's coming.'

'Just keep breathing, love,' said the nurse, distracted by

something that was happening outside the door. 'We've just got something to deal with out here.' And then she disappeared again. Through her pain Mary heard shouting in the corridor but instead concentrated on the cruel strip light on the ceiling as if it was a beacon showing her the way. The shouting became louder and she made out a man's voice. She heard '*Fuck you!*' and '*Let me through, you bastards!*' and other swear words, but it meant nothing to her because of the pain. She couldn't understand who was shouting and why. All she wanted right then was him beside her, holding her hand. She leaned her head to one side and a tear slipped down her cheek as she remembered the first time she'd ever set eyes on him, standing on that bridge in Ashton, over a year earlier.

She hadn't really wanted to meet him but her mate Maureen had persuaded her.

'Come on, Mary, what's up with you? Don't you want to meet a fit lad? He's not from 'round here.'

'Where's he from then?' she'd asked.

'Ashton-under-Lyne,' Maureen replied in a magical whisper, as if Ashton was the most exotic place in the world. Mind you, compared with Denton, where Mary had spent all her life, it was. Even a town five miles away offered excitement and new possibilities. 'And he's like 18 and he's dead grown-up and he's got this nose that's like dead flat, like a shark. He's been in loads of fights and he's not like other lads round here. He's right nice. And he knows stuff.

Come on, Mary, come and meet him. He said that I could bring a friend and he'll take us both out.'

Mary listened as she pushed her hair back into place, using the window of her parents' sweet shop as a mirror. Maureen only wanted her to go along because she was too scared to go and meet him on her own. 'OK then,' she sighed, as if it were a big hardship. 'If it makes all that much difference to you, I'll come.'

She and Maureen were the adventurous ones at school, and Mary had always been up for a bit of excitement to ease the dull life that her parents wanted her to live. Mary dreamed of something other than the terraces of tiny, red-brick houses in Denton, a working-class hinterland a few miles from the heart of Manchester. She dreamed of anything else but her parents' shop. Through the window she could see Tom Nolan, her father, serving a customer, his bald head shining, a healthy, sturdy man who loved his beautiful daughters. Of the three strong-willed, intelligent Nolan girls, Mary was the youngest and the most easily led. She didn't want to work in the sweet shop or a bakery and had already got herself a part-time job as a magician's assistant at the local theatre. At the tender age of 15 she was far too interested in the glamour of the stage and the adult world for her father's liking.

'Eh, brill,' said Maureen, doing a little jump. 'I'll meet you tomorrow and we'll get the bus to Ashton. We're to meet him on the Guide Bridge at four o' clock,' she said, skipping off happily. Mary caught her father's eye through the window and waved at him. For some reason, the description of the boy that Maureen had given her had piqued her interest more than usual. That night she conjured up a mental picture of him, which meant that as she approached the windy bridge the next afternoon with Maureen, she couldn't help but be a little nervous. As they walked along, their smart, pointy shoes clacked against the pavement and their linked arms were tensed together in excitement. David stood alone on the middle of the bridge with his hands shoved in his pockets, braced against the wind, watching them. It was a chilly day, rain was drizzling and, from where Mary stood, Ashton seemed as depressing as Denton. As they got near, the boy took his hands out of his pockets, removed the cigarette from his mouth and blew smoke into their path before flicking the butt down into the river below.

'All right?' he said, and gave them a broad smile. 'I'm David Vaughan. Or Dave the Rave, as people call me.'

Mary smiled cautiously and looked away. Something about him made her heart flutter. It wasn't really the way he looked, which wasn't exactly what she had imagined. He was dressed in tight corduroy trousers with the waist button missing, a windcheater and a shirt that was up-to-the-minute mod fashion but a bit grubby. His hair was messy and cut awkwardly around his face, which wasn't handsome, but rather chiselled out of some rough stone and then maybe sand-blasted to leave smooth, round cheeks. His eyes seemed sad but were soft and kind at the same time and his nose – well, Maureen had got that part right. It was flat and crooked, as if it had been punched a fair few times and then some. Mary stole another look at him and summoned up the courage to speak.

'I'm Mary. Mary Nolan.'

He wouldn't stop looking at her for some time, and it was as if something was happening around her. Maureen chattered away happily enough as the three of them left the bridge and went to get a cup of tea, but Mary was thinking only about David. They went into a café and David entertained them both with stories of parties that he had been to, music he liked, his ideas and ambitions. He seemed to know everything and he was *18*; he was *so old*. When Maureen went home for her tea, Mary stayed. She was too scared to look at him for too long, instead focusing on his hands, which were big and grubby with long fingernails that were full of paint. They seemed to tell a thousand stories. He told her that he was an artist. That he wanted to get out of Manchester and study at art school. He didn't seem like any other man in the world. He had ambition. He explained to her that his mother had abandoned him when he was a baby and that his grandmother had brought him up.

'Mum did come back once when I was about four or five,' said David, sipping his tea, now dark with a skin that had formed in the time he'd spent chatting. 'All I can remember is that she came back to get some clothes, she said, and I followed her up the stairs, then she came out of the room and instead of picking me up, she pushed me down the stairs and I fell. I couldn't understand why she wanted to hurt me.'

'At least you had your grandma to look after you,' said Mary, trying to find a way through the pain she felt on his behalf.

'My nan was as mad as a hatter,' said Dave, staring deeply into his tea. 'Instead of giving me dinner, she'd cut pictures of food out of magazines and put them on my plate.'

Mary bit her lip, trying to contain an overwhelming urge to touch him, to take away his pain. He didn't know who his dad was, he said, and tried to not look particularly bothered about it either. But this vulnerability had made her even more attracted to him. Everything he did, whether it was stirring his tea or lighting a cigarette, was strong and certain, but his eyes told another story. David walked her to the bus stop, all the while never taking his eyes off her face.

'I want to draw you,' he said finally, as the bus came along.

'Me?' she said, staring at the pavement. 'Why do you want to draw *me*?'

'Because you're beautiful,' he said, grabbing her face in his smoky, grubby fingers and staring even harder. As he did so her face caught the light of the streetlamp and showed off her huge, round, blue eyes – oval-shaped, elfin eyes which shone like a beacon. Eyes that might melt a thousand hearts. He let his gaze roll over her face, which to him was as pretty and delicate as any doll that could ever be crafted. He felt as if he'd seen all the girls that Manchester had to offer but Mary was something else. There was something about her petite beauty, the slim figure and doe eyes that had instantly driven him crazy. She wouldn't have looked out of place among the models he'd seen in fancy London fashion magazines.

'Go on then,' she said, breaking free of his hand and mounting the bus. 'I'll meet you tomorrow if you like.' As she watched him through the window, she felt butterflies and knew that she was in love.

The next day they met, and he was true to his word and had turned up with his charcoals to set about drawing her. She was impressed with his skill and tried to keep still and avoid the temptation to fiddle with her hair.

'I'm gonna get out of here soon. I'm gonna go and live in Cornwall with other artists, then I'm gonna apply to art school in London and I want you to come away with me,' he said in his thick north Manchester accent, and then he kissed her. They kissed for a long time with closed eyes and through the dream she brought his rugged face into view. His dusty-blond hair felt like straw but to her it was manly and impossible to resist.

Soon enough her parents started to get concerned that she was often out late and skipping her homework. One day, in the small front room of their neat, two-up two-down house, they confronted her.

'So who is he? This new lad of yours.' Tom stood by the

MARY AND DAVID

window and looked out at the row of red-brick houses opposite, his blue eyes sparkling. Mary had got his eyes, and the prettiness of her mother, Betty, who sat next to her on the sofa. What she hadn't inherited was their contentment with what they had.

'He's called David... Why, Dad?'

'Because he's standing over the road smoking,' said Tom with a worried look at his daughter. 'Why don't you go and ask him to come in?'

Mary did as he said and soon David was drinking tea on their sofa, while her mum and dad stared at him.

'So what's your trade, lad?' said her father after a few minutes of awkward silence.

'I'm an artist.'

Mary winced inwardly as she knew that wasn't the answer her father was after. She saw him bristle.

'An artist? You need a proper job, lad.'

'Why should I? Just so the bloody government can take it all in tax? Fuck that.'

David stood up, drained his tea and strode out of the door, leaving Mary shell-shocked and her mother twiddling her rosary and saying her Hail Marys. Her father went to the window and watched David retreat with an air of satisfaction.

'You are not to see him again, Mary, you hear me?' he said sternly. Tom had brought up his daughters to be spirited, taking them out on bicycles into the Pennines, but not so spirited that they disobeyed him. Mary grabbed her coat and marched towards the door. 'Why not? Just 'cos he doesn't have a job? That's no reason to stop seeing someone,' she shot back, angrily slammed the door and ran to catch up with David. Suddenly everything looked too small to Mary: her parents wanted her to be a good Catholic and go to church rather than live her life.

She continued to see David despite their disapproval, until one day Tom got the ammunition he needed to end his daughter's relationship once and for all.

He brought it up the next day at dinnertime. She got in late and plonked herself down at the table, immediately noticing that her mother and father were not eating but staring straight at her. Tom cleared his throat.

'This lad of yours. I told you to stop seeing him.'

'You can't make me stop seeing him just because *you* don't like him,' said Mary, defiantly popping a chip into her mouth which nearly fell out again as her father brought his fist down hard on the table.

'You are to stop seeing him, because the lad is married. He's only got a bloody wife, and she's only got two kids by him as well.'

Mary stayed silent, looking fastidiously at the meat on her plate. She noticed that her mother, dressed neatly in a sweater and skirt, wasn't eating either.

'But he loves me,' Mary said as she tried to absorb the news.

But Tom wasn't going to back down. 'You're not even bloody 16 years old,' he went on. 'You should be

MARY AND DAVID

concentrating on your education. You'll stop seeing him or you'll be sent away. You can go and live with your cousins in Torquay.'

She fled from the table to her room to cry and later on she snuck out to meet David and buried her head in his arms. It seemed as if they were the only two people in the world. She asked him about his wife, even though she didn't care if he had a wife, or ten million children. All that mattered was the two of them.

'I'm not with her no more,' he explained, as Mary looked at him inquisitively. 'It were a stupid mistake. I got married and had kids. I was too young, I'm still only 18, and I want to be with you.'

Mary looked up at him in despair. 'They told me that if I see you again they're going to send me away to Torquay,' she said as she felt his strong heartbeat through his nicotine-stinking windcheater.

'Good,' he said defiantly. 'Let them.'

The next week, as she was put on to a train at Manchester Piccadilly station, her mother gave her a final hug in the aisle of the carriage while Tom heaved her suitcase up on to the luggage rack. He looked at his daughter awkwardly before hugging her himself.

'It's for the best, love, you'll see. Give us a ring when you get to Torquay. Your cousins will help you get some work as a waitress, OK?'

Mary nodded dutifully, hoping they didn't look at her too closely and see what she was really thinking. As the train eased out of the station she waved one last time and then turned to watch Manchester slip away past the window. No sooner had the suburbs disappeared than the train pulled into Stockport station. Doors clanked open and new passengers bustled on board, accompanied by a burst of chilly air.

'Come here often, love?' said a familiar voice. David plonked himself down next to her and kissed her full on the lips. She smiled a smile of utter faith as he threw his bag on to the rack next to hers. 'Next stop St Ives,' he said, grinning devilishly. She didn't understand why her parents hated him because the more powerful he seemed, the deeper she slipped into love with him. To her, David was a charming, kind, talented and exciting man. He made her life worth living.

She would soon find out that their fairy-tale elopement wasn't going to be the idyll she had dreamed of. Once they reached St Ives, Mary phoned her parents and lied, telling them that she had arrived in Torquay safe and sound and that she would start to look for work as a waitress the next day. They didn't need to know that in fact David had checked them into a boarding house as Mr and Mrs Vaughan and they would be living in blissful sin. Before long Mary did find herself a job as a waitress, at a seaside restaurant called the Captain's Table. Her good looks meant people always wanted to employ her because she attracted custom in the right way. David started to paint and fit into

MARY AND DAVID

the local artists' community. But she soon found out that trouble had a habit of following David. He told her more about his eccentric grandmother and she got the feeling that he had been a wild kid, only saved by his talent for art and drawing, which he had been encouraged to pursue at school. His teachers had praised his talent, and for Mary it was this talent and those words 'I want to draw you' that gave David his charm.

It wasn't long before their playing at Mr and Mrs in St Ives was interrupted, when Mary was spotted in the restaurant by a friend of her parents from back home in Denton. Mary knew this meant trouble and told David as much later that night, when they were in bed.

'They'll grass us up. I'll have to go back to Denton. What are we going to do?'

'Fuck 'em,' said David in his usual careless tone. 'We'll just run away again.'

'Where to?' said Mary, having just starting to settle into life in Cornwall.

'London, of course,' said David, lighting a cigarette. 'I'm bored here anyway.'

Soon enough they got the phone call from Mary's parents telling her to leave David and come home immediately. Soon afterwards Mary and David were on the train to London.

After the picturesque, seagull-filled cobbled lanes of St Ives, getting off the train in scary, dirty London seemed as terrifying as it was exciting. In time they found a small bedsit above a shop on Tyndale Road, off Upper Street in Islington. It was September 1964 and David was full of enthusiasm, applying for a scholarship to the Slade School of Art on the advice of artists he'd met in St Ives who had seen his talent. He was accepted by the school, one of the most prestigious in the country. Mary used what little money they had from her waitressing and odd jobs to spruce up their single room. She idolised David's style and copied the fashions and trends she saw about her on the London streets, experimenting with velvet and glitter and bits of fabric. It was the beginning of the Swinging Sixties and London was the centre of the universe. They were now bona fide grown-ups, sharing their first home together.

Soon, though, Mary missed a period. She realised that now they were going to be playing at being parents too. Not knowing what to do, and having no one to call, she'd found the self-help book on pregnancy and read it thoroughly, both scared and excited about telling David. Scared because she had realised that, along with his charm and talent, came temper and violence. The kind, lovely, handsome, rugged bloke she adored was tainted by the chaos of his strange upbringing. He was constantly getting into fights and often wouldn't come home because he'd been in a drunken brawl and got himself arrested. By then she was scared too, because she'd cut all ties with her old world. After she hadn't come home from St Ives, her father had told her that they were going to disown her. She couldn't go home now, and she knew no one in

MARY AND DAVID

London. Apart from the baby growing inside her, David was all she had. As much as she loved him, she had started to fear the stranger inside him. For all his tenderness and passion, there was a part of him that wasn't *her* David.

Mary lifted her head from the pillow, disturbed by another agonising contraction. She couldn't believe that so much had happened since that meeting on the bridge just over a year before, and now she was about to have a baby of her own. There were two or three nurses in the room, all busy staring up between her legs.

'One more push, Mary, love! That's it!' one of them said and smiled at her.

All Mary could see was stars in front of her eyes as pain blurred her vision. A red mist flooded her head as blood and sweat mingled in her nose and mouth. Then suddenly she cried as she heard a high-pitched scream and her baby was plopped on to her chest.

'It's a girl!' said the nurse excitedly, examining the scrawny little scrap. Mary stroked her baby and the relief from the agony brought forth more tears.

'What are you going to call her?' asked the nurse, cleaning the afterbirth from the puce-coloured little body. Mary stared at her child in rapture and wonder, full of the most weird feeling of belonging and peace. 'I'm going to call her Sadie.'

The shouting in the corridor had started up again and

two of the nurses left the delivery room. Mary began to recognise the man's voice. It was David.

'I just wanna see my fuckin' daughter!' he roared, then there was more scuffling.

'You can't go in there, sir. You're not legally her husband. It's against hospital rules. If you don't leave now I'll call the police and have you arrested,' said the nurse.

'I don't care about the fuckin' rules. I'm a bastard and so is my little girl.'

Suddenly the door to the room was flung open and David fell through it, followed by a nurse and a hospital porter who desperately tried to pull him out again. He broke free, stood up, stared at Mary and approached the bed nervously. She closed her eyes, not knowing whether to laugh or cry. She didn't want any trouble but all the same he was all she had. As David leaned over and took a long look at his daughter, so small and perfect, his eyes hardened, making him look older than his 19 years, and he pulled back.

'She's not fuckin' mine. Look at her,' he said finally, turning away.

'What? Course she's yours,' said Mary, confused. 'Look at her again.'

David glanced once more at Sadie, who was covered in dark hair, almost black, so unlike his colouring. He just couldn't accept that she wasn't made in his image. This child, born of a beautiful mother, didn't look anything like him. Baby Sadie was yellow with jaundice and she looked more like a little foreigner than he could take.

MARY AND DAVID

'I don't know who she looks like but it's not me. She's not mine,' he said, walking out of the room. As he did so the nurses and the porter tried again to grab him but he shook them off. 'It's all right,' he said. 'I'm going and I won't be back.'

He didn't come back the next day, or over the next ten days, and the nurses, seeing Mary had no one else to care for her, let her stay as long as possible until eventually they needed the bed for someone else.

'But where can I go? I haven't got any money,' Mary said as they explained that she'd have to leave the hospital. She knew she would have to go back to Tisdale Road, and on her own. As she packed her things around Sadie in a little Moses basket that the nurses had supplied, she knew she had to track David down. But first she needed clothes: she had only what she was standing in, and nothing for her baby. The hospital arranged for her to go to a charity shop for young mothers to get kitted out with second-hand babygrows. She picked out a few nice ones and, with Sadie safely installed in the basket, she boarded a number 19 bus outside the hospital.

It was 3.30 in the afternoon and the bus was crowded with schoolgirls eating crisps and swapping tales. Mary found a seat on the top deck and, with the basket on her lap, watched the chattering lasses all around her. It was strange to think that they were her age, and that just a year earlier the same preoccupations that they had, like who was kissing whom and what to wear for the school disco, had also been hers. Now she was worrying about other things, more serious things, like whether she had been abandoned by her lover and if she was alone in the world.

She entered their house and approached the bedsit fearfully, only to find that the door was locked and her key didn't work. She sat on the stairs and waited, occasionally checking on her sleeping baby. Eventually a neighbour came in and started to climb the stairs.

'Don't suppose you've seen my Dave, have you?' said Mary hopefully.

The neighbour stopped to get her breath and looked at her sorrowfully.

'He moved out, love,' said the woman. 'But he left a forwarding address for post and that. I'll fetch it for you, flower.'

Mary picked Sadie up and held her tightly. Her worst fears seemed to be confirmed. Didn't Dave love her any more? She had to find him, and quickly. If she could just show him how pretty his daughter was... She made her way to the address written in scruffy handwriting on the scrap of paper: 110 Gloucester Avenue, just a few streets away. It was a room above a garage and on the other side of the road were some big, posh houses. The place was run-down, needing more than a lick of paint. She took a deep breath, picked up the Moses basket and went inside. It was ten days since Sadie had been born and she was unsure what kind of welcome she would get, but still Mary

MARY AND DAVID

was determined to keep their little family together and make everything right with Dave.

Like the street door, the door to David's flat was not locked, so she pushed it open. He was fast asleep in a single bed in the corner of the room. The single bed hurt her like a knife through the heart. She shut the door behind her and, taking Sadie in her arms, approached his sleeping form.

'David, it's us, your family. We're back,' she said, her heart thudding as he stirred. Instead of looking at her he simply rolled on to his other side.

'All right,' he said before drifting back to sleep. She breathed a sigh of relief and knew it was all going to be OK. He was just scared too, she told herself. It was all so confusing, but she hoped that before long he'd grow to love his daughter like she did.

And she was proved right, for soon things returned to the way they had been in St Ives. Now that Sadie had a more normal colour and David could see his daughter was a beautiful impish little creature, his heart melted. They got by on the few pounds that came in here and there. But, despite David's devotion to Sadie, he remained erratic. His art kept him out until all hours, trying to make money or fighting or partying. Whatever he did, he did obsessively. To Mary's regret, it seemed that he wasn't able to be the David she loved all the time. There were demons inside him that she was too young to understand. He didn't understand his demons either but now he had a new life in Camden Town, the epicentre of everything hip.

While pretending to themselves that all was well they were living separate lives, and Mary had no choice but to accept it. She missed her family back home and decided that perhaps the sight of their granddaughter would melt the ice and her parents would take her back into the fold. She convinced herself that taking Sadie and David up to Denton in a show of familial joy and harmony would make it clear to her father and mother that she was a responsible parent, not just a wayward teenager with a baby. So back up north they went, with little Sadie as a peace offering. At first things went to plan. Everyone behaved as David was offered tea and cake and Betty fussed around Mary and the baby, while Tom chatted awkwardly to the father of his granddaughter.

'She's beautiful,' cooed Betty as Mary and David looked on proudly. More relatives arrived and Sadie was roundly admired.

'She looks like a Nolan,' said somebody. 'A proper Nolan. She's got the Nolan expression.'

David's face turned cold and it was as if day had become night in his mind. His baby wasn't a Nolan, she was a Vaughan. This family who had tried to ban him were taking ownership of the only thing he loved and he wasn't going to stand for it. He stood up and the air about him seemed so thick with his enemies that he choked on it.

'She doesn't look like a fuckin' Nolan,' he said, grabbing a bottle of tomato ketchup that was on the table next to the food so carefully prepared to welcome him. 'She looks like me.' And with that he launched the bottle through the window, sending glass everywhere. He stormed out into the street and disappeared.

Inadvertently, Mary had given her parents all the fuel they needed to get her back. They swung into action, banning her from leaving the house and filing a request with a solicitor to make Mary a ward of court for her own protection. The full force of the Catholic religion was called upon too, and when the local priest appeared he was consulted in great depth. Sadie would be offered for adoption.

David was not seen again after the tomato ketchup incident. He returned to London and Mary knew that whatever happened she had to get back to him. Despite his violent outbursts, he was all she knew, and even though she was so alone, London was now her home. But more than anything, there was no way she was giving up her baby. Not ever. Soon afterwards, when Mary was back in her old bed in her old room in Denton, she decided enough was enough. So what if Vaughany was a lunatic? She and Sadie belonged with him. She got up, packed as quietly as she could, and with Sadie in her carry-cot, let herself out into the dark street.

David

Until 1967 home for Mary and David was the studio flat in Gloucester Avenue, and life returned to normal. Or as normal as it ever was for them. There was still no money but somehow they got by. Mary started to make clothes and David painted the room. Dylan and the Beatles were on the record player and Mary earned what she could by customising any old piece of cloth or furniture into the latest fashion. If David came home with a television set she would brighten it up by sticking glitter round the edges. She made sure they had trendy clothes and David walked about in the latest drainpipe cords, his hair styled like the lads in the Beatles, with Chelsea boots and neckerchiefs, usually covered in paint. He liked what he saw in the mirror, liked the fact that he looked harder than the southern jessies. He was stocky and pretty stout, but he walked tall as he strutted round the Slade, making both friends and enemies. There he met two like-minded artists, fellow northerners who had a business together customising furniture. Douglas Binder and Dudley Edwards were part of the über-hip London scene, and once David was in with them he was on his way. Binder and Edwards were already making pieces of furniture for Princess Margaret and Lord Snowdon and the latest pop sensation, the Beatles.

David started to customise furniture himself, painting it with the rainbow effects and vivid colour combinations of the psychedelic art that groups like the Rolling Stones used on their album covers. One day he brought home a chest of drawers that he'd found in a junk shop and started to paint it outside in the street, while the strains of the Stones' new blistering single, '(I Can't Get No) Satisfaction'

MARY AND DAVID

streamed out of the studio's window above. He stripped off his shirt, rolled a joint and was resting a while, when he heard footsteps coming downstairs. It was Mary, with Sadie in her arms.

'Can you have her out here? She's driving me mad upstairs,' she said, dumping Sadie next to him. He gave his daughter a quick kiss and Mary smiled at the two of them, rubbing her belly. She was pregnant again, due in a month, but despite her size was dressed in the latest fashion to hit the streets, an outrageously short skirt called the mini, popularised by the designer *du jour*, Mary Quant. She went back upstairs and David carried on with his work, keen to get the final touches on the drawers. Sadie played happily next to him and he couldn't resist picking up his notepad and charcoals and drawing some quick sketches of the child. As he was finishing them, Sadie toddled over and stared at the drawings.

'Daddy, I brought it to you,' she said, looking straight at him with an intensity that seemed from another world.

He took this as a sign – like something magical. He scooped her up and whispered in her ear. 'Yes, my angel, you did bring it to me. You – only you brought it to me. You brought me my art, you brought me everything, because you are a gift from God sent from Heaven to save me,' he said to her, suddenly possessed by the absolute conviction of his own talent. He picked up the chest of drawers and dragged it across the road to the bottom of the stone steps that led up to the front door of one of the posh houses. He lit the spliff and went up to the front door and rang the bell. The door was opened by an unshaven young man, good-looking, dressed in the latest fashion.

'Yeah?' said the man, looking him up and down.

'Hey, man, I'm David, I live over the road.' He stuck out his hand for his neighbour to shake. 'I know who you are, man. You're David Bailey, the photographer.'

'Yeah, so?'

'Well, I wondered if you wanted to buy this chest of drawers.'

Bailey looked past Vaughany and down at the drawer fronts, magnificently painted, but something else caught his eye. A grubby little child with a mop of black curls had appeared and was trying to climb on top of the chest. The child was wearing nothing but a pair of baggy red pants smeared with dirt and a string of beads round its neck. The little nose was covered in snot that was also smeared across her entire face and in places had become encrusted with the remnants of food.

'Is that your little boy?' said Bailey, smiling.

Vaughany smiled back and shook his head. 'It's mine, yeah, but it's not a boy. That's Sadie.'

'Fuck me,' said Bailey. 'I seen her playin' over there and always thought she was a boy.'

'Tell you what,' said Vaughany. 'If you like the chest of drawers I'll do you a deal if you take some photos of her.'

'Done,' Bailey said with a grin.

They shook hands on the deal and Dave Vaughan made

his first sale – not to mention the fact that little Sadie Vaughan was about to be photographed by the man who would become one of the most famous photographers of all time. In the end, David Bailey didn't actually take the chest of drawers from him but Dave was still bursting with pride to have agreed a sale to such a prominent man. He would soon make contact with Bailey's circle of friends. Before long, his art and furniture were the must-have items among the cool London set, his work was being written about in trendy magazines and, to cap it all, he received a commission to paint Paul McCartney's piano in his trademark motif, a haze of swirling psychedelia. He had money and a degree of success he could never have dreamed of. Soon he started selling his furniture in Lord John of Carnaby Street, the pinnacle of fashion, where they asked him to paint a huge mural above the shop window, an offer he gladly accepted. On the second day of the job Dave got a friend to help him and the two of them hung suspended in a painting cradle 30 feet above the street, lashing on colour and singing at the tops of their voices. Dave started to dance in time to the music coming from inside the shop, but something must have given because the cradle, dangling on ropes, dropped on one side and he slipped, and his mate Mick, a big, heavy bloke, fell on top of him as the whole cradle crashed down to the street below. People screamed and one of the sales staff ran out to help.

'Fuck me, are you OK, man?' said the shop assistant as he surveyed the wreckage. Dave was wedged in below

Mick, who had squashed Dave's head against the cradle, which had been the first thing to make impact with the ground.

'Aaargh … *fuck* … uhh … *fuck*,' said Dave, holding his head as someone pulled him upright.

'We better get you to hospital, man,' said the assistant and then called for an ambulance.

'Fuck off,' said Dave, ignoring the searing pain in his temples. He ran his hands over his head, and, apart from a couple of grazes and a pounding headache, he appeared to be intact. He had an aversion to hospitals and would rather chill out with a joint, so he sat and had a smoke as he waited for some of his mates to turn up and take him home. Unfortunately, his mates had another idea and took him to a party, where they dumped him in an armchair in the corner.

'Drink that,' said one of them, giving him a shot glass. After 15 minutes Dave was unable to move, his entire body splitting into millions of particles and floating out into space. His mates sat and laughed at him.

'What've you fuckin' done to me?' Dave asked, holding on to the chair for his life.

'LSD, man,' said one of them. 'We thought you needed a good trip.'

Dave would have got up and knocked them out but he couldn't move. For two days and nights the nightmare continued and when he finally got home, Mary was hysterical with worry.

MARY AND DAVID

'Where the fuck have you been? Lord John told me you'd had a fall and hurt your head,' she shouted as he collapsed into bed, a shell of his former self. 'I checked all the hospitals.'

'I didn't go to hospital.'

'But what about your head?'

'What about it? It's bloody fine, woman.'

It wasn't fine, though. After the bang to the head and the LSD, Dave fell into a slough of depression. Everywhere he went he saw the acid trip repeating itself. His happiness at his newfound success was replaced with aggression and paranoia. It was as if something had gone pop in his head. Work fell away and even the once-friendly David Bailey stopped inviting him in for a drink after he had started a fight with one of the photographer's influential friends. Slowly ,the work and the money dried up. All Dave had was his precious Sadie, and now he would just sit at home and brood.

'Fuck you all. You're all conspirators against me,' he said to himself one day, grabbing a tin of red paint in one hand and scooping Sadie up with the other. He went off up Primrose Hill, to the iron bridge over the railway line that headed north. He didn't care that it was late and that Sadie was dressed only in her pants. When he was with his little girl, everything was all right. While he painted the bridge red, with big, violent swipes of his brush, Sadie picked the pants out of her bum and toddled off to play in the dirt. He didn't stop until the entire bridge was painted, and then lit up the spliff that was behind his ear, standing back to admire his handiwork. It was ten at night and he knew that he should have taken Sadie home to bed. He felt momentarily responsible before picking her up and taking her off again.

'Fuck the lot of you,' he said under his breath. 'Fuck the world.'

He kissed Sadie's dirty face and whispered in her ear, 'You don't have to do anything they want you to do. You don't have to conform. You just gotta be what the fuck you want to be.'

A 'black Maria' crawled to a stop at the end of the road. The officers inside the police van appeared to be admiring his artistry and then the doors opened. David didn't stop to hear what they were saying; he ran with Sadie in his arms.

'Oi, you!' they shouted, but he didn't slow down, dashing through the streets, away from the law.

A month later, on 12 May 1967, Mary gave birth again at the Whittington Hospital, to a little girl called Sunshine. She seemed to Mary to be a little blonde cherub, not at all like the impish, dark Sadie, but still the perfect finishing touch to their little family. But David was becoming increasingly erratic, no money was coming in and things were again at breaking point, especially with another mouth to feed. Besides, Vaughany was always getting arrested, particularly after his recent spate of red painting. It wasn't just the bridge: it was the houses of certain people that he disliked. He'd taken to breaking in and painting their entire place red. Soon the couple got an eviction order for non-payment of rent on Gloucester Avenue and they had to move out in the middle of the night with everything they owned. They went to stay with a friend of Dave's called Pete Blackman, who was in both a reggae and a steel-and-skin band. The Blackmans had two kids of their own and only a small flat. Things were not ideal.

'Fuck all this living in a tiny room. Let's just piss off out of here,' said Dave one afternoon as they lay on the single bed in the Blackmans' spare room. Beside him Mary struggled to get Sunshine into bed and pacify Sadie. She kissed them both and repeated the rhyme she told them every night like a mantra to keep them safe: 'Night-night, Sadie. Night-night, Sunny. Night-night, sleep tight, don't let the bedbugs bite.' But, as she tucked the blanket in tight around them, Mary sensed trouble in David's words.

'Piss off to where? We haven't got any money,' she replied.

'Formentera. Ibiza,' said Vaughany, putting Dylan on the record player before stretching out on the bed again. 'Sun, sea, sand and sex. The scene is supposed to be fuckin' great.'

'But how? It costs money to get there.'

All the while, Sadie was wide awake, staring at her parents and repeating the night-time mantra they were so fond of.

'Night-night, sleep tight, don't let the bedbugs bite!' she

said with an impish smile. Mary tried to shush her but Sadie just carried on. 'Night-night, sleep tight...'

Dave stroked his daughter's hair and stared ruefully at the wall.

'Fuck it all, we don't need anything. Fuck society. Why should we live according to rules imposed by them? We'll sell everything we own and just go.'

'Go in what, Dave? We've got nothing,' said Mary, sensing that he was building up to one of his money-making plans that usually ended in disaster.

'You don't have to worry about that. You just start getting the kids packed and ready to go.'

Vaughany never disappointed when it came to surprises and a few weeks later, having spent the proceeds of the sale of all their worldly possessions, he turned up outside the flat in a rusty old single-decker bus. 'Let's go and drop out, love,' he said as he leaned out of the window. As usual, Mary had no choice but to swallow whatever words she'd prepared and just smile.

CHAPTER TWO

Sadie Vaughan

*S*napshots *of me. Running. Always running. Pictures of places like photographs blurred by motion.*

Running... I was in a pair of big strong arms. The arms belonged to my father. We were running fast, the wind playing with my hair. I was covered in red paint... Someone was chasing us...

... running down Primrose Hill laughing with my dad ... there was a chair at the top of the hill ... I was sitting on it. Some men were taking photographs of me sitting on it...

'Sadie! Put those back!' *I was running out of the door of the shop and down the street... I was swallowing the biscuits as I ran ... behind me my mother was shouting and trying to grab me. I ran but she was faster. She caught me.*

'You are a VERY bad girl,' she said. 'You will take those biscuits back. We don't take things without paying.'

...Running down the stairs at my birthday party. Children at the table, people singing 'Happy Birthday' to

me. Three candles but I was running away from the cake because I was scared... There was a bear in the room and he was chasing me and I was crying. The bear followed me down the stairs, I couldn't run fast enough. I heard people laughing upstairs, adults laughing and singing.

'Happy birthday, dear Sadie!'

But the bear was trying to catch me, I ran out of the front door and into the street, looking around for someone to help me but I froze because the bear was above me now. I gripped my arms together and felt wee come down my legs. The bear started to laugh and then his head came off and I screamed. My dad's face was where the bear's head used to be. He picked me up. His breath smelt of something very strong. He was swaying from side to side. He drank from a bottle. A bear holding a bottle.

'You don't have to run away, Sadie, it's only me in a bear suit. Don't be scared, love.'

...I fell on the ground when I was playing. I was bleeding ... my eye was cut... My father scooped me up. He worried. He ran down the road with me ... running to the doctor and blood splashed on the pavement... I watched my blood drip on to the pavement, a luminous red trail behind us...

...Running through a field ... hard to run in that long dress, picking up the hem, I took Sunshine's hand. Sunshine was dressed in a long dress too and we both wore big hats like cowboys wear. The sun was strong, beating down, and something was singing but not a bird, something else. We

were running away from something. Sunshine was crying and I was scared. We were running away from something… Daddy was behind us … we were scared and he was shouting … we were running…

We were all in a big bus, Sunshine was on my mum's knee, Daddy was driving and music was playing. Daddy sang along to 'Like a Rolling Stone' by Bob Dylan.

'Say goodbye to Primrose Hill, kids,' said Mum as we drove past the park. We said goodbye to Primrose Hill, goodbye to Camden High Street and goodbye to the big train stations at King's Cross and St Pancras. We drove past endless fields in the dark after London and then we got to a place called Dover. Everyone stared at us because we were in a big bus that Daddy had painted up in lots of colours, and everyone pointed at it. Then we drove on to a big boat. Then we did much more driving, with a lot more fields. Sometimes we slept and would wake up and we were still driving and so me and Sunny would go back to sleep again until one day I woke up to see snow-capped mountains on every side of us. The bus seemed small as it went up and up further into them. Mostly what we ate for lunch and tea was bags of nuts and chocolate milk. When we stopped for a pee in the middle of a field we were so small and the mountains were so big and the sun was burning hot even though there was snow up there on the tops. As it got later the sun got hotter and back in the bus the seats started to smell of burning.

Eventually we crossed more sea and as the sea got deeper and bluer the sun got hotter and hotter and then a big island appeared and Mum pointed at it and said it was called Formentera. In Formentera there were no telephones or gas or electricity and because of this it was paradise, she said.

Outside the bus me and Sunny played in the hot sun. Mum and Dad went to get big bottles of Calor gas and set up the cooker. It was like having a kitchen outside the bus, and each time they cooked there was a special smell from the gas. And we had a kettle that whistled when the water boiled. At night we lit a gas lamp and sat around listening to special insects that made a noise by rubbing their back legs together, and all the world seemed to live outside with us. Mum and Dad would put us to bed and sit outside and we'd listen to their voices murmuring and laughing while we slept in the bus. Dad would come in and kiss us.

'Night-night, sleep tight...'

'Don't let the bedbugs bite!' I'd shout in return and Dad would smile.

After a few days we would pack everything up and go to another campsite and unpack again and it was like playing house. One day in Formentera the sun got very hot, like an oven, and the ground was so hot it hurt when you walked. Mum said it was something called a heatwave and everyone was in a bad mood because it was so hot. I walked quickly on tiptoe across the dirt to where Sunshine was playing under a sheet tied to the front of the bus to make shade.

SADIE VAUGHAN

There was a stone building next to us and in front of the bus in every direction were yellow fields. I played with Sunshine's hair, putting flowers in it and humming a song, trying to drown out the sound of Mum and Dad shouting at each other.

'We haven't got any money for food or petrol.'

'We've got fuckin' cheese!' he said, pointing to a large, round, mouldy thing sitting on the table under the awning attached to the bus. 'We'll be all right for days with that.' He marched off to gather some firewood. Meanwhile me and Sunny carried on playing until my attention was caught by a stray dog that had stolen up to the table and was grabbing the cheese in its big jaws.

'Dad, Mum! The dog's eating the cheese!' I screamed, but not quickly enough. The dog heard me and ran off with the whole thing.

'Bastard!' said Dad, chasing the dog and throwing a bottle at it. Mum came out of the caravan and started shouting, 'What about the kids, David? We have to eat.'

'All fuckin' right, woman! Shut up, for fuck's sake!'

Mum and Dad went back inside the bus and carried on shouting at each other. There was the sound of something breaking and Dad shouted even more. I grabbed Sunshine's hand and yanked her away from the bus. She didn't want to come but then something came crashing through the window and I pulled her even harder. I wanted to be away from the bus. I pulled Sunny through the field, away from the bus. My dad came after us, running after us, but I didn't want him to follow us. I wanted to run away...

We were back in London again, and I was two years older. A woman in a white coat came into the room and shut the door. Mum stroked my head as I lay on her lap with my head against her breast. The coughs racked my chest and each time I buried my head deeper into Mum's velvet coat while she rubbed my back, the cutting pain like a knife inside me. The woman in the white coat had a long tube dangling from her neck. She held the tube and there was a metal bit at the end.

'I'm just going to listen to your chest with this, OK, Sadie?'

I hid further in my mother's coat until the doctor gently but firmly coaxed me round to face her, then placed the metal against my bare flesh. Its cold hardness was strangely nice.

'Can you cough for me, Sadie?'

I coughed. Sometimes when I coughed there was red in it. Mum cried when that happened. She stroked my head and I lay against her and listened to the murmuring of her voice as it vibrated through her breast against my ear. She was talking to the doctor about things I didn't understand, but I listened anyway.

'And Sadie's father? Can't he help?' asked the doctor.

'We've split up. He's going a bit barmy so I've left him 'cos he's too mad,' Mum replied tearfully.

'So where are you living now?'

'We were travelling like, you know … we've been in Ibiza for nearly two years. We were living in a bus, but we ran out of money so we came back… All over the place really.'

I kept seeing me and Sunshine running through the fields, the sound of Dad breaking things in the bus, Sunshine crying and me wanting to run away from him. Daddy wasn't a normal daddy any more, he was scary.

'Well, Sadie is quite poorly and she needs to be admitted as a patient,' said the doctor finally, after writing some notes.

'What is it?'

'It's a condition called bronchiectasis in the left lung. Basically it means the lung isn't working properly and if she gets a cold or chest infection it can be very serious indeed. She needs to stay in hospital to be treated and then you'll need to find her somewhere to live that's warm and dry.'

Mum hugged me tightly, whispered goodbye and cried because she couldn't stay with me, then a nurse came and put me in a bed on my own. Days passed and Mum didn't come and collect me. The nurse told me Mum was busy trying to sort out a place for us to live and that she'd be back to get me soon enough, but I knew what it meant. No one wanted me. I was alone in a hospital because I was too much trouble. After three days a nurse gave me a toy soldier made out of wool.

'That's for being a brave soldier,' she said as she tucked me in and left. I hugged the soldier tight; he was all I had.

Soon after, Mum did visit me but she said I couldn't go home with her till I was better. Apparently home was now with someone called Roy, a friend of hers. A week later Mum said I was well enough to go home with her and Roy came in his car to collect us from the hospital. Sunshine and I sat in the back and Mum was in the front with Roy. I heard some more long words.

'They say she's got something called double pneumonic bronchiectasis.'

'Fuck, man,' said Roy. 'And what about Vaughany?'

'Don't ask me. I don't want to see him again,' said Mum.

When we got to Roy's I knew at once that things weren't good. Mum cried all the time. Daddy came round sometimes but no one would let him in and he shouted and pushed people and smashed things up. I heard someone say that Mum had applied to make me a ward of court so that he couldn't come and see me any more. My chest got bad again and I coughed and coughed and everything hurt. Soon Mummy wouldn't get out of bed and I heard Roy whispering that she was having something called a nervous breakdown. Roy and some friends of Mum's took me to the hospital again.

One day soon Mummy was smiling again. And I felt better. My cough had gone and even the doctors at the hospital kept smiling, telling me I was 'getting better'. Mummy was laughing with a man she called 'Frosty'. He picked me and Sunshine up and took us to the park. He had big, safe arms and we never ran anywhere like we did with

Daddy. We walked. Frosty reminded me a bit of my dad because he was a painter too. He was from Manchester as well. One day I heard Daddy talking about Frosty and it wasn't very nice.

'Bloody Frosty's a bastard,' he said to Mummy, kicking a door. 'He used to follow me about the place in Ashton, a snotty-nosed little kid hanging on to my coat tails. Now he's bloody followed me down south and he wants my bloody family, the little bastard.'

Frosty's hair was different from Dad's hair. It was short and curly at the front and very long and very bushy at the back, but it was also the same as Dad's hair because it always had white paint in it. His clothes were all covered in paint as well but Mum told me he wasn't an artist like Dad. He had something called a proper job: he was a painter and decorator. Soon we moved out of Roy's house into a new house, at 178 Haverstock Hill. It was big and scary but we lived on just the second floor. Mum said that the flat belonged to the council and needed 'doing up'. When we moved in Frosty moved in with us and painted the front door yellow. Mummy painted the walls purple and red and started to make us new clothes. The song 'You're So Vain' by a singer called Carly Simon was in the charts and Frosty bought the record and we played it over and over, all of us singing along.

'Guess what, girls,' said Mum excitedly one day. 'Me and Frosty are getting married! Today! And you two are going to wear special dresses.' I jumped up and down on

Mummy's bed, which was in one corner of the front room. In another corner lived our parrot, Clover, and he started squawking and pecking at the iron bars, so I put a blanket over his cage to shut him up. In the same room we had a big glass tank with fish called carp in it and they sucked my fingers if I put them in the water.

Mum had measured us for our dresses – mine was black velvet with a lace collar – and started sewing the hems, when there was a knock on the yellow front door. Four or five people came in, all dressed in velvet flared trousers and carrying bottles of wine and a guitar. There were always lots of people in our flat, and music and parties. The people in the flats around us got angry and shouted through the floor and called us names. Sometimes they called the police.

Soon Frosty arrived in his suit and we all got ready. Me and Sunshine were bridesmaids, so we were given bags of rice and confetti to throw at Mummy and Frosty. Mummy looked really pretty in her dress and after they were married we all had our photograph taken in front of Camden Town Hall.

Dad moved into the flat next door to us. Mum called his flat a squat. She kept crying and shouting at him to leave her alone, but I liked having Dad next door because he gave me a lot of attention. Sometimes I didn't like Sunshine because she was the baby and because she had blonde hair she got all the attention. When I was ill with my cough I got all the attention and I liked it. When I didn't get attention I would say something bad, like my dad, and then people told me off.

Sometimes Dad painted things like 'I love you Sadie. You are God' on our front door and Mum and Frosty got angry about it and had to paint over it, but he kept doing it. Lots of times Dad tried to come into our flat and Frosty had to stop him, which led to a fight. Once I asked Mum why she couldn't get back with Dad and she hugged me and said, 'Because your dad is too mad. I need Frosty, to keep your dad away from us.'

One day Daddy came to the door and put me on his shoulders and took me out for the day. He forgot my coat and my shoes but he said it didn't matter.

'Thing is, Sadie…' He was talking as he smoked with one hand and held on to my legs with the other. I held on to the sides of his face. I loved being on his shoulders because I felt so tall and everyone looked at me. 'I wanna show you something,' he said.

We went to see a car that he had painted. It was called an AC Cobra and was shiny and expensive-looking.

'This car is gonna make me famous and I'm going to America because they are gonna put it in a big store called Macy's,' he said.

'Why?' I asked. 'Why?' was mostly all I said when I didn't understand what anyone was saying.

'Why? Because it's 19 fuckin' 69 and you are the Jesus child!'

'What does that mean?'

'It means,' he picked me up and hugged me, but it wasn't a normal hug: he was holding me so tight I thought all the air was going to be squeezed out of me, 'that you are God. You are my connection to God, you are everything and it's time that the world saw your power,' he whispered, breathing hot breath into my ear. My dad had a really serious look on his face. He wasn't making a joke like he did a lot of the time.

Then we went to a building called the RCA and Daddy decided to make a giant cross.

'What's that?' I said, trying to balance on one leg.

'It's a crucifix, and you are going on it. Because you are God, Jesus and the Holy Spirit.'

I shrugged my shoulders and went to play with two other children who had arrived with a friend of his. My knickers were big and baggy at the back and I felt silly. We were outside and it was cold, so we ran about while Daddy built this thing he called a crucifix. A bit later he put me on the crucifix and told me to stand there for as long as I could and then he would buy me an ice cream. Soon people were stopping outside the building to look at me and Daddy was talking to them about it.

'See – I am sacrificing the thing I love most in the world in the name of art.'

Then he opened a book and started reading to me. Soon I got tired and asked Daddy if I could get off the crucifix thing and put the rest of my clothes back on. Daddy took me home and Mum shouted at him.

'You've been gone with her all day and she didn't have a coat and she's sick!'

'She isn't sick. She's God,' said Dad, staring at me.

'You are crazy. You've gone mad. You are off your head on drugs, aren't you?' said Mum.

Dad grabbed me and tried to take me out of the front door. Mum held on to me and I was caught in between them.

'Sadie comes with me. She is my connection to God,' he said, gripping me tightly.

'You're off your head on drugs.'

Frosty pushed Dad while Mum took me out of his arms. I didn't know what 'off your head on drugs' meant but I knew that Dad was like that a lot.

I went into my room to play with Sunshine while the three of them carried on arguing. Things always ended like that.

In September that same year I started school at Primrose Hill Primary. The building was a big old place with shiny floors that squeaked when you walked across them and smelt of disinfectant. I loved it because it was clean. Everything was always the same there. That was strange because at home nothing ever happened the same. My best friend at school was Katie Maude and we made the boys chase us around the playground. Two of the boys who played kiss-chase with us were called Sam Mendes and David Miliband, and they wore smart clothes. Most of the other kids made fun of me because my clothes weren't smart like theirs. 'Your mum and dad are hippies and you don't have any money, nur-nur-na-nur-nur,' they would sing.

One morning I woke up and heard Dad's voice and my heart leapt. I hadn't seen him for a while because he'd done what Mum called a 'disappearing act', as he did sometimes. It sounded like the shouting was coming from outside the house and I looked out of the window, my hot breath steaming up the glass and I wiped it aside. Down on the grass below our flat Daddy was painting a chair.

'Why don't you just leave us alone? You disappear for weeks and then turn up with no money.'

'I'm getting money. I've been working at a lithographic printers. We're doing incredible work, printing and designing posters for the Stones and the Beatles. I'm working with a geezer called Martin Sharp, we're right in at the heavy end. It's gonna be massive.'

'What about your kids? They need stability.'

'I live next door, don't I?'

'I don't want you to live next door. I want you to stop creating havoc.'

'Well, that's fuckin' tough, 'cos I'm not leaving the kids.'

My heart was beating very hard and I realised that I had better get myself ready for school because Mum might be too upset to help me when she came back upstairs. I dressed quickly, slipping on my favourite velvet dress. Mum had made it for me the week before and its best feature was that it had heart-shaped pockets. No one else at school had a dress like that. In the mirror I could see my face. I turned my head from side to side. My hair was getting longer and wasn't as dark black as it used to be. I had twinkly eyes and everyone told me that I was 'pretty'. I didn't really know what that meant – it just meant people smiled and touched my cheeks a lot. I twirled round and round in front of the mirror in my dress, watching my reflection, then I stopped turning because no one was there to watch me. I went back to the window and opened it and leaned right out.

I could see smoke rising from a cigarette Dad was holding. After a moment a waft of pungent tobacco smoke hit my nose, making it wrinkle. Sometimes Dad's cigarettes smelled of something stronger. I once found some of it under my bed and it smelled the same and Dad told me it was just flavouring and was called pot.

'For Christ's sake, woman, can't you leave me alone?'

I went back into the front room and got up on a chair and found a bowl and poured some cereal. I got the milk from the fridge and started to eat. I wondered when they would come back up and notice me. I heard footsteps beating up the stairs and Mum ran in and smiled.

'Are you upset with Daddy?' I said as she kissed my forehead.

'No, love. Just talking, that's all. You look so pretty in that dress,' she replied in her soft Mancunian accent, and gave me a smile that reassured me for a moment.

I tipped up the bowl and drank the milk straight from it.

Mum was packing my school bag and had tears in her eyes and was trying not to cry. As she moved about the room I slipped downstairs. Dad was sitting on the half-painted chair drinking tea out of a pint glass. He was wearing a pair of velvet trousers that were tight at the top and went out at the bottom like a bell. Everybody had trousers like this that flared out and fluttered in the wind. He had paint in his hair like snow but it was hard and dried white paint. His collarless silk shirt billowed in the wind, the swirly multi-coloured patterns on it making it look like a crazy flag, and his spiky-toed Chelsea boots were flecked with red paint.

'You've got paint on your best trousers, Dad,' I said, trying my best to sound adult.

Suddenly aware of my presence, he spun around and gave me a huge smile which lit up his handsome face, took the cigarette out of his mouth and put it to death under his shoe.

'Eee, ecky thump, it's my Sadie! Hello, my angel!' He picked me up, kissed me and held me tight. His shaggy beard scratched my skin and he smelled of something that I knew meant he'd been out all night. It was the smell of something sickly sweet, something wrong. I looked into his eyes and the black bits were really small, like pin pricks. But I didn't care what he smelled of as long as I could bury my head in his chest and breathe his smell in deep.

'Shouldn't you be getting to school?'

I played with his thick, scratchy hair, which was long and uneven round his face.

'Can't I stay and help you paint?'

He put me down and picked up his brush, dipping it in the red paint and applying it in an expert swirl down the arm of the chair. I'd lost him. I tugged on his arm.

'Daaaaad?'

'What, my angel?' He sounded distant, as if he'd already forgotten me.

'I don't want to go to school because Mrs Mawson shouted at me. She was really really horrible to me and she made me cry.'

He stopped painting and looked at me, concern flooding his face.

'She did what?'

'Made me cry.'

He gathered me to him and gave me a hug. At that moment Mum appeared with my coat and school bag. She grabbed my hand without a word to my dad and dragged me away. Dad turned immediately to the chair and stooped to dip his brush in the paint again. We walked the whole journey to my school in silence, Mum gripping my hand warmly and giving it an occasional squeeze, though I could tell she was miles away. It was September and the new school term had only just started but already the leaves on the trees in the streets were turning brown and dropping off. I kicked the leaves as I walked, a sort of distraction from Mum's silence. They made a crackling messy sound. I made Mum leave me at the gate and shrugged off her kisses. I didn't like her walking in with me because some of the other kids laughed at how she dressed. All I knew was that Mum was different from the other mums in that way. She wore long, brightly-coloured kaftans, and that day she was wearing something called a poncho which was made of wool.

'Mum?' I said, concentrating on kicking leaves. 'Can I have a grey dress?'

'Why do you want a grey dress?' said Mum, hurrying me along.

'Because all the other girls have grey dresses and it's made by Polly Esther.'

I had to run a bit to keep up with her.

'Can I have a Polly Esther dress, Mum?'

Mum wasn't really listening, I could tell. 'It's polyester, love, not Polly Esther. And no, you can't have one because it's a man-made material and is against the natural planet,' she said, adjusting her poncho. 'Besides, we can't afford it,' she added, stopping to lean down and kiss me before I ran through the school gates. I got to my classroom just in time before Mrs Mawson took the register. She moved between the rows of chairs giving out exercise books. She gave me a little smile which was more of a line than a smile and as she walked away I stared at her bottom because she always wore tight trousers, so you couldn't help it.

'Now, class, I've put some sums on the board and I expect you to get on with them in silence.'

I studied the blackboard, chewing the top off my pencil. Rudi Davies and Katie Maude, who were sitting behind me, started giggling and Rudi tapped me on the back.

'Like your dress, Sadie,' she said.

'Thanks,' I said, going back to my sums. Then I got another tap on the back.

'Did your mum make it?'

I heard them giggle but I carried on with my sums.

Around midday the smell of disinfectant gave way to boiled cabbage and we filed down to the lunchroom. Rudi and Katie stood in front of me in the queue and both were given meat and potatoes on their plates.

'Just potatoes, please,' I said.

Rudi and Katie looked at me and giggled again.

'Why don't you have some meat, Sadie?'

'We don't eat meat,' I said, repeating the words I'd heard my mother say so often in cafés and restaurants. 'We're vegetarians.'

They giggled again. I went to sit at another table, far away from them, with some boys who I knew wouldn't snigger at everything I did. After a while the boys got up and ran to the window, craning their necks for a view of something that was happening outside.

'Look!' said Simon Tucker. 'There's a fight in the playground! Quick! Look!'

Rudi, Katie and the rest of the kids ran to the window. 'Look! There's a man, he's trying to hit Mrs Mawson,' said one of them.

Shouting and swearing could be heard coming from the

playground. Something made the hairs on the back of my neck stand up. I continued to eat my potatoes, which I'd wrapped up with peas and carrots in a lettuce leaf.

'Look at that man,' said a girl called Fiona. 'He's got paint all over him.'

I stopped eating and remained frozen to the spot.

The shouting from outside became louder. Other male voices could now be heard.

'Look, there's a policeman!'

Eventually I got to my feet and went over to the window. Outside, in the playground of my school, Dad was being held by two men teachers as he kicked and struggled to get at Mrs Mawson, who was holding her face as if she'd been hit.

I ran outside but stopped as soon as I got near them. In fact I stood behind Mrs Mawson, so that Dad couldn't see me. His face was red raw and raging. 'You fuckin' shout at my daughter and I'll fuckin' have you! You hear me, you silly bitch?' By now two policemen were trying to get him down on the ground and two more male teachers were trying to comfort Mrs Mawson.

'Daddy, stop!' I said eventually, feebly, feeling as if my skin was dropping off in pain, sliding off like ice cream. Everything went hazy and dizzy. I was floating on a cloud. Away from there. At last Mrs Mawson noticed me and, looking at me, whispered to the male teacher. 'Someone take Sadie back to the classroom,' she hissed. 'She shouldn't see her father like this.' Everyone stared at me kindly as the teacher took me to the staff room and gave me a glass of milk.

'My dad,' I said after a while. 'He's really nice usually but he's not very well, that's all. It's not his fault.' These were the words my mother would say to me, so I just repeated them while the teacher took my hand.

The air was chilly – it was the winter of 1970 and I was five and a half – as I stood on top of the stall at Camden Market and did a twirl in my Victorian lace dress, lace gloves and high leather boots. I shouted at the top of my voice, 'Come and get your antiques here! Lovely dressing table and chairs!'

Mummy laughed and carried on dusting all the things she had on the stall. Things that me and Sunshine had crammed under our bed because there was no other space for them: old pots and bottles and china jugs. I got off the stall and went to look at myself in an old mirror that was leaning against a chair in front of the stall. The mirror was also for sale; everything was for sale. In the mirror, I adjusted my cowboy hat, which Mum had put a silver star on. She had the stall all day for the whole weekend so that we could make enough money to do the shopping at the supermarket. Sometimes we didn't have enough for things like bread and breakfast cereal and then Mum would find whatever she could to feed us.

I loved the market at Camden. There were loads of stalls and people shouting and selling their stuff. It smelled of incense and there was the delicious aroma of someone cooking lentils. Sometimes we had a stall at Wembley market and Mum would sell the clothes that she made. She was busy on the stall and I could run about and no one told me off. I didn't like being told what to do. Not at school or anywhere. After Daddy had come to my school I had to be careful what I told him. Mum said I wasn't to tell him anything about school, and I knew that if I did, he would be down to sort it out. After he hit my teacher he was banned from entering the school, but he knew how to get my attention. Walking home after school, I would look up at a brick wall and see big red letters painted there which read: 'I LOVE YOU SADIE, MY ANGEL OF THE NIGHT'. He would leave me messages in paint on every wall on every street all the way home. At the same time I knew how to get his attention. If I told him anyone had been nasty to me, he would get angry.

On my sixth birthday Katie Maude and I had a joint party on Primrose Hill. Katie looked almost the same as me: the same blue eyes and chubby cheeks, a turned-up nose with freckles on it and gappy teeth. Whatever I did, she did. But Katie's mother wasn't like my mum, who wore ponchos and wooden shoes and daisy chains around her head. She was called Mary, like my mum, but she was always neat and tidy and wore floral dresses designed by Laura Ashley. Katie's mother walked in a very upright way, like she was a ballet dancer. Anyway, Katie and I invited the whole class from school to the party.

'Let's make them all walk up the hill to our tree,' I whispered to her, cupping my hands round her ear. Katie giggled and grinned.

'All right then.'

So I started skipping and dancing up the hill, followed by Katie, and then the whole class of kids followed us. We felt like we had so much power when we were together. If I touched my bottom, everybody touched their bottom. If Katie rubbed her head, everybody rubbed their head. We looked at each other and laughed and led everyone to our special tree, which we called Tweedledee and Tweedledum and pretended was the centre of our kingdom.

Katie and Mary moved to a new house in Brecknock Road in Tufnell Park, because Mary was getting married to a man called Gary. I liked going to Katie's house because it was so different from our flat. Everything was clean and tidy and they had dinner at the same time every day. The floor was polished wood and they had a grand piano that Katie was learning to play.

'Are you staying for tea, Sadie?' Katie's mum asked me one day.

I nodded while I ran my fingers lightly along the keys of the piano, dying to push one in and make a noise but not wanting to get into trouble. At tea we all sat together at a big table and Katie's mum brought out this green thing that looked like an alien spaceship. Then she cut it open and light green gooey stuff came out.

'Would you like some, Sadie? It's an avocado,' she said, smiling.

'Is it vegetarian?' I asked.

'Very,' said Gary, pouring some red wine for him and Mary, then winking at me.

I looked down at the various knives and forks in front of me and the others looked expectant, but I had no idea which knife or fork to use or even how to hold them right. At home we just got on with eating any old how. Gary was nice. He always had a tan and wore really smart shirts. And he never shouted or got angry. There was also a delicious potato salad made with new potatoes, which were the same as old potatoes but much smaller and sweeter.

In their kitchen they had tiles on the floor that were made out of furry stuff called cork. The next time I saw Dad I told him about Katie's house.

'And they go to this shop called Habitat, where they get lots of new furniture from, and it's all shiny and new.'

'So?' said Dad, spitting a piece of tobacco from his teeth. 'It's all fuckin' shit, Sadie. It's all fuckin' capitalist bullshit. We aren't made to be wealthy. We need to hate them people, all them people and their bullshit.'

He went back to smashing up an old chest of drawers. I watched him do it, and as he smashed, it was as if he was smashing all the magic spells that I had woven in my head about how exciting and new life was. He blew all the magic away. I stomped off back upstairs. I saw the hate in his eyes. I was angry and I was confused, but he was my dad, and if he hated people with nice houses, then maybe I should too. Inside something felt wrong and hollow, as if there was a hole where the magic had been. The hole was like being hungry and I didn't know what to replace it with.

I got our record player from the front room and dragged it into my and Sunshine's room. Then I put on an old record and dressed up in some of Mum's high heels. I just wanted to fill the hole inside me, and by singing and dancing I invented a world where I could escape to and everything was created just for me.

I sang along to 'I Feel Pretty' from my favourite musical, *West Side Story*. I picked up a fan that I'd stolen from Mum's market stall and hid behind it. I knew the words of every single song from *West Side Story* so well I didn't need to listen to them. Performing like that was my favourite thing in the whole world.

Mum got pregnant again in 1972. The contractions came on quickly while I was getting ready for school, and she shouted at me, 'Quick, Sadie, go and tell someone to fetch Frosty. My bloody baby's coming!'

Me and Sunshine jumped on the bed, too excited to go to school or do anything. Frosty and Mum went to the hospital and someone came to look after me and Sunny. The next day Mum came home from the hospital with a basket containing my new baby sister. Jessie was the most beautiful thing in the world and had bright red hair. We all hugged her and Mum and Frosty. Mum laughed and told us that when the baby had come out covered in blood, Frosty had fainted. The sun came out and the little flat looked bright and cheerful. It all made sense: I was dark, Sunshine was blonde and baby Jessie had red hair. We were all different but now made up a team.

Soon after Jessie was born Mum needed to start working and making money again. This time it was with the Sidewalk Theatre Company. She was part of the team and took us along with her to watch and listen while they all rehearsed plays and sang and danced. I immediately knew that I had to join in and show my dance moves to some of the other performers.

'Sadie, stop it,' said Mum, putting her finger to her lips. I realised that everyone was watching me. Some man who everybody called 'the director' was looking at me like he didn't like me, because I was dancing right where the adults were doing 'a scene'.

'Go and sit down,' hissed Mum, making sideways movements with her head that I knew meant 'Scram!' I sat down in a heap and put my head in my hands. All I wanted to do was be in the play. Instead I watched as the director and the costume person told everyone what to do and wear and where to stand. I drifted off back into my own fantasy world where I was the centre of attention, and hummed a tune.

Not long afterwards Mary Maude noticed that I like to

sing and dance and offered to give me lessons. She knew all about dance and ballet and everything.

'Can we start now?' I asked excitedly, loitering by the piano in Mary's house.

'Not now, Sadie,' she said. 'After the summer holidays.'

I went home in a huff. Mary and her family were going away for the school holidays and there was nothing I could do. When I got home I found Mum and Frosty loading up a little red car, shaped like half an egg, that he had bought for her.

'It's called a Citroën 2CV,' said Frosty, standing back to admire it, his wiry, curly hair going mad in the wind. 'And it's gonna get us all the way to Africa.'

'Where?' I said, trailing my finger down the side of the car.

'Marrakesh, to be exact,' he replied, slipping a cassette tape into the player next to the steering wheel.

'Will we be back in time for school starting again?'

'Dunno. God knows. Maybe we'll never come back,' said Frosty, grinning.

As dusk fell over Camden me and Sunshine were loaded in the back, Mum and Frosty were in the front and baby Jessie was wedged between me and Sunny, in a washing-up bowl. We drove through the light-streaked streets of London to the sound of Bob Dylan. It reminded me of going to Formentera in the big bus and driving for ever, through fields and countries, all the time it getting hotter and hotter. This time we were all in the little red car. Sure enough, as we drove and drove it got hotter, and eventually we had to fill the washing-up bowl with cold water so that Jessie wouldn't be too hot. When we began to climb up into the mountains the heat in the tiny car made me and Sunshine argue and fight. We argued over the chocolate milk and pinched and kicked each other until our skin was purple and bruised. After crossing the sea for the second time we arrived in a country called Morocco. More driving and we arrived in a big city called Marrakesh.

It was a place that I couldn't stop looking at, but everything seemed scary as well, and that made me have to look even more. As we drove further into the city the roads became narrower and ended up like alleyways and we got stuck in a traffic jam behind a man who was whipping a donkey that was pulling a wooden cart.

'Poo, that stinks,' said Sunny, staring at the cart as it went on ahead of us. As it rolled along I saw people come out of doorways and throw buckets of mouldy rubbish and vegetables on to the cart. The strangest thing about it was that a little boy was balanced on top of all the rubbish and he was sorting through it even though it was smelly, and his T-shirt was so dirty you couldn't even see the colour. The boy chattered away to the man whipping the donkey in a language I didn't understand. However much I wanted to look away from the boy, I couldn't.

Old men with piercing eyes and rough black skin, and thin like skeletons, leaned against walls smoking. They all had gaps where their teeth should be and as our car crawled through the tight streets behind the donkey they stared back at me and smiled, revealing still more endless black holes where teeth should have been.

'We'll bloody park 'ere,' said Frosty, swinging the car into a tiny space between two battered, even older cars, and we all got out, glad to stretch our legs. But suddenly I felt scared to join the alien world I'd been watching from behind the safety of the car window. Once outside, among the strange and bad smells, it was much worse. In places the air smelled like the incense that Mum often burned at home but mostly it just smelled like dead animals, but almost sweet and sickly.

As I walked along between Mum and Frosty, who were carrying Jessie and Sunny, I felt like all the men were boring holes in me with their yellow eyes. One of them, who looked like a wizard in my book, beckoned me to him. I dropped back, behind Mum, and stood and looked at him. He was standing in a doorway holding something in his hand that was gold and shiny. As I went nearer I turned to see Mum and Frosty looking at some bowls in a nearby shop. The man called me to him and when I went closer he touched my skin and hair, as if he had never seen a little girl before. Then I noticed what he had in his hand – it was a snake. I turned away and ran to where Mum and Frosty had been just a second ago, but they were no longer there. In a panic, I ran, looking behind to check the man wasn't following me. As I looked up, all the market traders were smiling at me from above, and then a hand grabbed me. I was being taken, against my will, by a strange, toothless man. I stopped in my tracks and my head went woozy.

'Sadie!' shouted Frosty, leaning down to scoop me up. 'Don't get lost, lass!' he said, and I clung on to him for dear life. He carried me into a huge open space, like a square, with hundred and hundreds of stalls. There I began to relax and soon wanted to explore, so Frosty put me down. A very old man with white hair was playing a flute and in the basket in front of him was a little snake that danced in the air to his tune. Smoke rose from open fires where men cooked bits of red meat and chicken, and little children played in the dirt, not minding that it was full of bits of yellowing flesh and the insides of dead chickens.

A few days later, when we'd set up camp outside Marrakesh and had come back in to do some shopping, me and Sunny had lost a lot of our fear. Now we ran among the food stalls in wonder, looking at all the weird and often disgusting things that were being cooked. I didn't mind the wiry men staring or reaching out to try and touch me, because Mum had explained to us that they just weren't used to seeing children with such pale skin. They loved to touch our hair, especially Sunshine's, as it was golden like the sun. In the tiny alleyways full of traders' stalls – they were called souks –people sold everything you could possibly think of, and me and Sunny ran through them breathlessly, loving the strong smell of perfume that overpowered every other smell.

SADIE VAUGHAN

The only bit we didn't like about Marrakesh was trying to find a toilet. The first time we needed to go Mum pushed us through a broken door and on the other side – to our horror – was just a china floor with hole in the middle and walls spattered with faeces. We had to balance our feet each side of the hole and be careful to not touch anything at all.

Back at the campsite some friends of Frosty had arrived in a big convoy of cars and trucks. Me and Sunshine ran about as if we were liberated while the adults wandered around in brightly coloured kaftans with headbands round their long hair. The men had long beards and all the other children we met were dirty and tanned. Soon we all had our clothes off and were playing around the water tap. I forgot about home and ballet and dancing, and the campsite became our new life. Mum would send me and Sunny to get the bread and milk from the shop. It felt so grown-up to have the run of the place. Most of the time none of the adults were bothered where we were. They spent a lot of time sitting in circles smoking something called dope and strumming guitars. All the kids on the site would just off and play as long as they liked. I liked to pretend that I was the mother and took all the pots and pans from the tent to the tap to wash everything.

Sometimes we went in the car to the big market square in Marrakesh, which was full of men arguing and eating. And we'd always see the man who made the snake rise up out of a basket with his flute. All the men looked at me as I danced along behind my mother, often only wearing a pair of pants, and I liked the fact that my dancing attracted a lot of attention, like the snake charmer.

We'd been at the campsite quite a long time and everything seemed OK, but then Mum and Frosty started arguing. There wasn't enough money to get anything to eat.

'I want to go home,' Mum said to Frosty one day. 'We've been away nearly three months. The kids need to go back to school.'

Frosty got annoyed and drove off in the car and left us. Mum sat and cried and so we just waited quietly, hoping that she would stop soon and tell us what we were going to do. Later Frosty reappeared in the car.

'Get in then. If you want to go home we'll go,' he said moodily, and we quickly packed up the tent until no trace of our life in Morocco was left. Our wonderful, free life at the campsite had vanished into thin air and now we were all grumpy and sad.

Back home in London, the arguing got worse and I longed to see my dad, who had by then moved out of the squat and disappeared again. Eventually he turned up to see me and I jumped into his arms. My present for going back to school was a new toy called an Etch-A-Sketch.

'Look, Dad,' I said proudly, showing him the red-framed screen on which pictures would appear as if by magic when you twiddled and twirled two white buttons. 'I can draw pictures.'

'Who got that for you?' he said, lighting a cigarette.

SADIE VAUGHAN

'Frosty did,' I said, not looking up as I sketched a cat. Then he grabbed the screen from my hands and threw it across the room. It hit the wall and fell to the floor with a clunk. I ran to see if it was OK but the grey screen was cracked and I knew at once it couldn't be mended.

'Fuck toys,' Dad spat. 'I can teach you everything you need to know about art. You don't need expensive toys to tell you anything.'

By now Mum was arguing with Dad, so I ran out of the room. Frosty was nowhere to be seen. All I wanted was for it all to stop.

When the next school holiday came round me and Sunny were put on a train to Manchester, to stay with Granddad and Grandma. Mum and Frosty weren't even talking to each other, so I was pleased to get out of the way. As I sat on the train and watched the worries of London slip away, I fell asleep. When I woke up I was excited to see – soon after we passed lots of dark bridges, red-brick streets and warehouses – that we were pulling into the station in Manchester.

We jumped out of the train and into Grandpa's arms. He twirled me through the air and then carried me to the car. Grandma was waiting at home. As we drove down their street I passed the children that I played with each time I went back there. I loved that all the kids were still there even though I had been away. The streets of Denton looked all the same. Peel Street looked like every other street. Everyone smiled, people said hello and everyone still lived in the same houses. No one ever moved. In London everyone moved house all the time.

The polished front door with the brass knocker opened and Grandma stood there. She was all soft and comfortably dressed, with a golden brooch pinned to her wool cardigan and her chubby arms open to hug me. I buried my head in her, smelling her smell and loving her round, huggable figure. She always smelled of old-fashioned face powder, the smell that I smelled in the empty powder compacts that Mum found in antique shops. All of a sudden I felt safe. Grandma and Grandpa's house meant proper family meals and walks and doing everything the way it should be.

Every time we drove up there with Dad or with Frosty, we would run out of petrol or someone would lose the keys and we would be lost somewhere, cold and hungry, for hours. But when we got there Grandma would make up for it by cooking a hotpot and giving us snacks of potato cakes and Eccles cakes. I would pretend to serve cocktails out of the proper little cocktail bar that they had in the corner of the room. I tasted a yellow drink called Advocaat that looked like custard. It was delicious at first but then it made me sick.

I would sit in front of the open coal fire in the front room and play with the assortment of neat and tidy fire implements that stood by the hearth. One of them was in the shape of a crocodile and I would poke and prod the coal while straining to hear what my gran and granddad were saying in the other room. They always shut the door against me when they were talking, but one day I heard Grandpa say, 'He came round and caused a commotion again, breaking things and shouting. Mary had to get the police. They've banned him from seeing Sadie.'

'He'd better not show his face round here,' said Grandma.

My stomach fell away. I knew they were talking about my dad. I hated feeling shut out. I got up and went to the mantelpiece to play with the tiny ornaments that Grandma collected. I got them all down and placed them on the carpet, lying on my stomach and playing with them. There were china dolls and glass dogs and elephants. It took my mind off what my grandparents were talking about, things I couldn't hear properly. It seemed like everywhere I went either I felt scared of my father and wished he was somewhere else, or, when he wasn't there, I wished that he was there to love me and care for me. How could he make me so happy and sad all at the same time?

Dad

Beard and twinkle, scratch and crinkle
Veins that spider, blood and cider
Blue and brown, that paints the town
Tea in pints, long dark nights
Tits and skin and smells of sin
Tents and cheese and socks and wheeze
Shouts and rants in underpants
Blood and fights and police and sights
Alone and smothered, undercover
Scaffold, on bridge, on LSD
Tea cosy on head, drinking tea
Picture pressed close to me.

CHAPTER THREE

Growing Up

Mum was with Frosty and things settled down a bit. My health was stable even though my bronchiectasis was a constant source of concern to Mum, but mainly it was calm because Dad had moved back up north and left us alone. He'd met another young girl of 16 called Anne who looked exactly liked Mum, and stayed with her in Ashton-under-Lyne. Things fell into a routine with Mum and Frosty and my sisters. In the half-term holiday we even went on holiday like a normal family. I watched the fields go by out of the window of the red, egg-shaped car. Dylan was again blaring from the stereo. Jessie was wedged between me and Sunshine and we were on our way to Wales. I was hitting Sunny, and Mum and Frosty were singing loudly.

'Mum, I need to have a wee,' said Sunny. Frosty sighed and pulled into a lay-by. There were a few houses nearby, but we got out for a pee, me and Sunny lifting our skirts, squatting down and baring our bottoms to the road, giggling. Mum and Frosty wandered off to share a cigarette and I got Jessie out and helped her have a pee too. I looked around at the unfamiliar landscape and sheep and fields. Frosty had told us that we were going to camp in a place called North Wales. We were going to stay in an old barn. When he described it he was so excited.

'It's gonna be great, kids,' he said. 'It's proper camping: no water, no electricity and no bloody man-made anything. We're going back to basics.'

At first it was really exciting but then the cold and wet weather started to get into our bones and halfway through the week I came down with a cold and Mum panicked because if I ever got a cold it might spread to my right lung and lead to a serious complication. My condition meant regular trips to Hammersmith Hospital for check-ups and appointments with specialists. I didn't mind because the doctors made me feel special and gave me treats. There were always lots of student doctors listening when the head doctor made me lift my gown and cough.

'Now, Sadie,' he explained to me in grave tones, 'you need physiotherapy on that lung of yours twice a day.'

'What's fizzioleprosy?' I asked, scared it was some kind of operation. This made Mum and the doctor laugh, then he explained that I had to hang upside down off the bed frame twice a day while Mum slapped my back in order to bring up all the green stuff that my bad lung wouldn't be able to clear on its own.

GROWING UP

So staying in a draughty barn in deepest Wales with only Frosty's wood fires to keep us warm wasn't good, and Mum soon started to fret.

'I think we need to get Sadie back to London. Her cough is getting bad.'

'We've only just bloody got 'ere,' said Frosty. Me and Sunny looked at each other: we could tell that a row was brewing. Sure enough, they were soon looking daggers at each other and we climbed into the car gratefully as we knew this was a sign that we were going home. We'd had enough of 'roughing it'.

After the half-term break and a big dose of penicillin it was back to school. This meant a return to routine and free school meals. Most of the other kids had pocket money but I had clothing grants and tokens for my uniform and for school trips that otherwise we would have had to pay for. Even though I had my friends Katie Maude and Rudi Davies, the richer kids would tease me in the playground. 'Why don't you ever have crisps, Sadie? Is your mum a hippy? Are you poor?' asked a plump boy called Ralph. I felt anger rising inside me and I pushed him hard in the chest. He fell backwards, while the other kids ran over and watched me beat him up.

'If you say another word about me I'll get my dad round and he'll duff you up,' I said as I stood over him, breathing hard, fists balled. Inside something felt good. Dad might not be around but it felt like his blood was in me. I didn't mind being a bully and using my dad to frighten people. I liked the feeling of getting what I wanted. I saw Denise Gallagher looking at me. She was part of a tough Irish family and had a cheeky but pretty face. Denise and the other tough girls gathered round and offered me their crisps. In one corner of the playground were the kids from the nearby council estate, in the other corner the kids from the big houses round Primrose Hill. I stood in the middle, not belonging to either group, then went into the toilet and stared into the mirror. I was so dark, with these bright blue eyes. I knew that some of the boys liked me and I liked that. But my clothes marked me out as a 'hippy' and a bit of a scruff. Denise Gallagher and Ruth Shawcross walked into the toilet and leaned against the sink next to me. 'Want to come to my house and play after school?' said Denise in her blunt cockney. I nodded seriously, not letting her see how desperately I wanted to be her friend. Despite being friends with Katie Maude and going to her house a lot, there was part of me that wanted to be with the naughty kids, and they were the ones who didn't have any money and felt a bit dangerous, like my dad.

Me and Denise started to be best friends. I would spend hours sitting in her room going through her older sister's make-up and putting it on. We started talking about boys. Ruth Shawcross came round and joined us. Ruth was really pretty – she had dark hair with a flick and she already had a figure and breasts – and the boys fancied her. We stood in front of the mirror and compared. My chest was totally flat and I thought I looked like a boy.

GROWING UP

'Hey, Sadie, you're as flat as a pancake,' said Ruth, looking at my chest.

'Pancake chest!' taunted Denise and they collapsed in laughter. I joined in despite feeling a bit annoyed at my new nickname.

'Who do you fancy at school?' Ruth said after she'd stopped laughing.

'Josh Nixon,' I said in as casual a tone as I could muster. 'I'm going to sit next to him on the school trip.'

The trip involved a coach ride to Windsor Castle and we all had to get up early and take a packed lunch with us. Mum managed to cobble together some hummus and crackers, which made everyone laugh as they tucked into their crisps and chocolate bars. All day on the trip I followed Josh around, and the more he ignored me the more I liked him. By the end of the day my heart felt like it was going to explode and I wrote him a note and passed it to him. It said, 'I LOVE YOU' and I watched his face as he read it but all it made him do was run away more. When I got home that night I ran straight to my bed and put the pillow over my head. It felt as if the world was ending. I pushed the pillow harder into my face, trying to stop myself breathing. Sunshine came into the room and stared at me, puzzled.

'Why've you got your pillow over your face?'

'I'm going to kill myself.'

'Why?'

'Because Josh Nixon doesn't love me.'

Two days later I had forgotten about Josh. There were new targets at school, like Stewart Smith, who had a mop of curly black hair, goofy teeth and smelt of sweat. He took me behind the bike shed and kissed me. At first I stood stock still and received his lips, all loose with saliva, slipping over my own like a fish. I could smell the cold air and the dirt on his hands and the sweat. When he'd finished he wiped his mouth and stared at me.

'Well? Did you like that?'

'It was all right,' I said. But really it had been more than all right. I liked the smell of him, the feel of his wet lips. I pulled him in for another kiss but he ran away. Who cared? Now I knew what power I had over the boys, suddenly I was ready to kiss them all. Especially the ones who were a bit dirty and had a musty odour. I didn't mind that. It was the way I was used to boys. It reminded me of my dad and the smell of him. My next crush was on the singer David Essex. Me and Denise Gallagher used to listen to his records in her room.

'Hold me close, don't let me go – oh no,' we whined along with the radio.

'Hey, guess what,' Denise said, jumping up excitedly. 'David Essex lives just near the park.'

'Really?' I said dreamily, staring at his face in a magazine I'd bought. 'I'm going to tell him I love him.'

The next day we searched all around Primrose Hill for his house. It seemed that his front door represented everything I ever wanted. After about four hours the door opened and

GROWING UP

David came out. He looked tired and had a sort of beard. He didn't look anything like he did in the magazine. Inside the house I heard kids shouting and got a waft of coffee. I stood and stared at him, no words came out and he just walked by, as if I didn't exist. I ran all the way home and got into bed, pressing the pillow to my face. Sunshine came in and stared at me.

'Are you trying to kill yourself again?'

'Yes.'

'Why?'

'David Essex doesn't love me.'

Sunny twiddled with her dress and frowned, leaving me to my despair.

Mum still worked at the street theatre and I was still keen on watching them perform. But then she got a job selling hot dogs at the Rainbow in Finsbury Park, which was a huge concert hall where pop bands played. I would go there with her, enjoying the smell of hot dogs even though I was a vegetarian; it was a nice, comforting smell.

'I'll sneak you in the back, Sadie,' said Mum, winking at me as she served a customer. 'It's Gary Glitter tonight.'

I smiled back in excitement and that night we watched as Gary Glitter strutted about the stage, dressed in sequins and leather. All the women were screaming and reaching out to him and he was touching their hands like he was God. I looked at Mum, the way she dressed and her make-up, and decided she was definitely the coolest mum I knew because she knew all about rock and roll.

Mum also took other jobs, anything to make more money, but because she was so pretty she got work as a film extra and Sunshine and I were really excited when she took us along to watch her perform. I kept dreaming that the director would call me over and put me in the film.

'You stay here and watch. Be good,' Mum said to us and we nodded obediently as she took her place on set. At that moment the star of the film walked by. I noticed people run around after her. She smelt different, she had this *thing*. I heard someone call her Glenda Jackson and I couldn't take my eyes off her. Mum was standing with a group of other extras. All I could do was stare at Glenda and the attention she was getting. I thought that Mum deserved to have a bigger role but I knew that I wanted to be like Glenda. I wanted to be the star.

I started to daydream of being an actress, especially at home when Mum and Frosty were listening to loud music and doing 'adult talk' and Sunshine or Jessie was crying. Alone in the bedroom I shared with Sunny, I would slip under my duvet and drift into my fantasy. In my daydream I was the star. My room would transform into a film set with lights and all my problems would melt away: the rows, the lack of money and the fact that, however bad he was, I missed my dad and the attention he lavished on me. When he was around it was like being loved too much, like being smothered by my pillow, but when he wasn't there, I missed his stupid jokes and his attempts to make me laugh,

GROWING UP

like walking around with a tea cosy on his head. School distracted me from my own fantasy world, and I particularly loved doing gymnastics. Firstly because I was quite good at it, and secondly because people watched me and I liked that even more.

One day in the gym I waited while the rest of the class and the teacher stood at one end of the hall. I was all on my own at the other end, my heart thumping.

'Come on then, Sadie,' shouted Mrs Daniel. 'Let's see you show the class how to do it.'

I ran towards the vaulting horse and thumped my hands against its furry leather, propelling my legs over the top, lost for a moment in time and space, seeing the faces of the children expectantly waiting for me to fall, before landing on the floor with a breathless shout as the air was knocked out of my chest. Everyone cheered and clapped. I righted myself, getting my breath back. I'd done it. I'd done a somersault off the horse.

That afternoon I ran all the way home, choking with excitement, and thrust a piece of paper in Mum's face. 'Look, Mum! Look!' She opened the letter and started to read but before she could finish I spoke. 'They say I'm good enough at gymnastics to attend the Sobell Centre.'

'What's the Sobell Centre?' asked Mum, trying to catch up with me.

'It's the centre of excellence for gymnastics. I'm going to start training there,' I shouted triumphantly. Mum hugged me. It was as if someone had shone a light on me. I was finally special, finally good at something no one else was good at.

'Can you believe it, Mum? Me getting extra lessons?' I was just little Sadie Frost who had free meals and uniform, but now the school were saying that I deserved extra tuition. This was the answer to why I'd always felt different: not because I was always ill or because we couldn't live in damp places for fear I'd catch pneumonia again, but because I had a *gift*.

One afternoon every week I left school early and took the number 29 bus to Archway tube station, then walked down Holloway Road to the Sobell Centre. I would stand in the changing room and admire myself in my bright yellow polyester leotard with a big Sobell Centre badge in the middle; suddenly I felt grown-up and independent. It was the floor work I liked best, because it was about dancing and I loved to move. But I also still wanted to act like I'd seen Glenda Jackson do and at home I increasingly isolated myself in my fantasy world.

It was around this time that I had to have more treatment on my lung, so I found myself back at Hammersmith Hospital. Mum left me there as she had to go home and look after Sunny and Jessie and I lay in the bed trying to keep covered up in the hospital gown that I wasn't sure should do up at the back or the front. Whichever it was, some part of me would stick out, usually my bare bottom. The ward was old, with paint peeling off the walls, and the high ceilings reminded me of my draughty school building.

GROWING UP

But even though the windows were wide open, I lay there and sweltered as I waited for the doctors to take me down for my operation. I was to have a camera put down into my lung so they could see what was happening. An old radio beside my bed emitted a crackling noise. 'It's official: 1976 is the hottest summer on record,' said a voice through the little speaker.

My stomach rumbled with fear and hunger. I'd had nothing to eat for two days, only liquids. Soon the nurses took me to the preparation room, where I was greeted by the anaesthetist. This was the only part I loved. I'd had a camera down inside me before and the anaesthetic had made me feel woozy and free. I'd been craving the feeling ever since. 'Now I want you to count down from ten for me, Sadie,' said the anaesthetist, smiling warmly. I smiled back, happy to have his full attention. Unlike all the other men in my life, this doctor made me feel safe and warm, and that was why I wasn't shaking in fear like most people waiting for an operation.

'Ten, nine, eight...' I tried to think of what came next...

When I came to I was back in my own bed in the ward. I felt scared and humiliated, all alone and in different clothes. Someone had changed me out of the gown into my nightie. A queasy feeling came over me. Where were my family and the doctors? I fell asleep and when I woke next there was a huddle of white coats round the bed, discussing me.

'We recommend that Sadie has her left lung removed – as a way of curing her acute bronchiectasis.'

I heard this, opened my eyes and panicked. Part of me wanted to sprint out of there in my nightie. When Mum finally arrived to see me I was a terrified wreck.

'Don't let them, Mum,' I said, gripping her hand hard, eyes wide with terror. 'Don't let them.'

All I could think of was my future career as a gymnast or a dancer or an actress, and I knew enough to know that girls with one lung didn't get to be gymnasts or dancers.

'Shhh, don't worry, love,' said Mum, hugging me. 'We won't do anything you don't want.' There weren't many things that I felt so strongly about, but I knew this was one operation I wasn't going to let them do.

Luckily my health improved and the talk of operations went away. At home, though, we were even poorer and had very few luxuries apart from the fish and a tank full of terrapins that Mum had got for us as a treat. The trouble was, the terrapins had a habit of escaping and we would find them crawling over Mum's duvet and under the bed.

'Mum? Can I have a flute? All my friends have musical instruments,' I said one day, removing a terrapin from the carpet and putting it back in the tank.

'No, love, I can't afford a flute. Ask your stepdad.'

'I can't even bloody afford the rent,' said Frosty, opening his newspaper.

'I can't feed us on air,' Mum snapped back at him, and suddenly Frosty put down the paper and gave her a cross look.

I sighed as I went back into my room and put on the

record player to lose myself. By this time I'd been at the Sobell Centre for six months and they were starting me on the bars. It was getting harder and I wasn't muscly or strong like some of the other girls and my interest was fading. My fantasies were more appealing than my family life and I started to perform for myself in my bedroom. I would pretend I was Maria in *West Side Story*. I turned the room into a boudoir, hoarding trinkets on my dressing table, along with old perfume bottles from Mum's antiques markets and Catholic artefacts such as rosaries and pretty pieces of card embroidered with the Virgin Mary that I got free from the church. I dragged the record player in there too, until the only thing that made it look like a children's room was the bunk beds that I shared with Sunshine.

'What are you doing, Sadie?' said Sunny, watching me from the lower bunk.

'Don't call me Sadie,' I said haughtily, imitating a posh Vivien Leigh accent. 'Call me Dame,' I said, dancing along to the music from *Gone With The Wind*.

Sunny got off the bed and left the room, her attention attracted by the noise of adults. I followed, and when I walked into the sitting room all the adults stopped talking and looked at me. Five or six of Mum and Frosty's mates had turned up and were making cigarettes out of special leaves and white paper.

'Hello, Sadie,' said one of them. 'What are you dressed up as?'

'Call me Dame,' I answered in that haughty tone, before spinning round to head back into my room.

I heard them all laugh and then someone said, 'What's she on?' I didn't understand, but I could see that they thought I was strange. I didn't care. At school I began to participate more in dance and drama. Katie's mother noticed that I had a talent for it and, because we couldn't afford ballet lessons, gave me tuition after school. I began to spend every night after school at her house, eating avocado and new potatoes and enjoying the calm, ordered life they led there.

'Have you thought of applying to the Italia Conti stage school, Sadie?' said Mary one afternoon as I had tea with the Maudes.

'What's stage school?'

Mary explained and after that, I wanted to do nothing else. At school the teachers also noticed that I was only interested in acting and dancing.

'I want to go to the Italia Conti stage school but we can't afford it,' I said glumly to my drama teacher one day.

'I'm sure you might be able to get a scholarship for talented children,' she replied, smiling kindly. I was nearly ten and the teachers were starting to get us ready for moving on to secondary school. 'But you'll have to do an audition,' she added, 'which you'll have to practise for. I'll make some enquiries.'

That night I flew home on the wings of some magical creature. I shut the door of my room and started going

GROWING UP

through all Mum's records. I pulled out the Beatles and put it on the record player. 'Here Comes The Sun' drifted into the air and I got up and started to make up a routine in front of the mirror. A few weeks later my school arranged for me to have an audition at Italia Conti. After that I spent all my time at Katie's house, doing dance routines with her mother in preparation for the audition. Mary was now called Mary White because she had married Gary White, and Gary was now something called a 'second AD' on a film called *The Hound Of The Baskervilles*.

'How would you like to be in the film, girls?' he said to me and Katie as we sat at the big posh table eating some posh food I'd never heard of. Gary and Mary had three courses for their tea, and it went on for ever. 'We need some girls to be extras.'

'Yes please!' we both said, almost jumping down his throat.

We hardly talked about anything else until the day arrived and we turned up at this huge mansion to start filming. Both of us were dressed in long white Victorian dresses and we felt like we were film stars, giggling and eating all the snacks laid out for the film crew while the main actor, called Dudley Moore, prepared for the next shot. Irene Handl, Kenneth Williams and Peter Cook were also on set and sat playing cards or doing the crossword.

That night I arrived home even more determined to do well in my audition. I stayed up past my bedtime and practised ballet until my toes hurt so much that I sat on my bed and untied my ballet shoes, wondering what the red stain was. As I withdrew my foot I saw that my big toes had started to bleed. As I watched the blood fill the gap between my nail and skin I was thinking only about Italia Conti and what life would be like if I got in.

Eventually the day of the audition arrived. I had prepared routines for the Beatles' 'Good Day Sunshine' and 'Here Comes The Sun' and 'Oom Pah Pah' from the musical *Oliver*. I noticed that the other girls waiting were dressed in expensive leotards and proper dance shoes. As they practised their routines I could tell they had all had plenty of tuition. Unlike me. I put on my blood-stained ballet shoes and took a deep breath. 'Good luck,' whispered Mum as I went in and danced my heart out, desperate to show that the combination of my home-made style and the Beatles was as good as any classical ballet they could watch.

The next week we waited and waited but no news came. I started to think that it was never going to come. I would get home from school and look at Mum's face and she would just shake her head. On the seventh day I got home and when I looked at her face she smiled broadly, but for a moment I didn't understand what she could possibly look so happy about.

'You got a scholarship!' she shouted, doing a little jump. I danced around the room, unable to take it in. I was to be a stage-school girl! At last I was going somewhere.

The end of term came at Primrose Hill but, instead of

being sad to leave, all I could do was die for September to come. We went to get the Italia Conti uniform from an old-fashioned shop which smelled of expensive fabrics and dusty curtains. For some reason the sales assistants spoke in whispers. In the mirror, wearing the school's heavy blue cape and boater, I felt like the most important girl in the world. It was as if putting them on made me forget all about Denise Gallagher, my other tough mates and kissing boys behind the bike sheds. I was someone else completely now. I was better.

The only person I kept in touch with from primary school was Rudi Davies, who was also going to Italia Conti. She had been with me since our first year there and I was glad to have someone to travel with. On our first day at our new school we met at Belsize Park tube station in our capes and got the Northern Line together. Rudi was shy and awkward and different from my other friends, in a good way, so I knew I would have a good ally in her. We got to Clapham North and stepped out on to the busy road, which seemed bigger and scarier than anything in Primrose Hill. And nothing was as pretty: the street was lined with little shops with flats above. Italia Conti itself was near the station, in Landor Road, and was much grander than everything around it, looking from the outside a cross between a big old house and a music hall. Once inside the building we felt so small, as older girls rushed past chatting excitedly.

'First-years this way, please!' shouted a lady with a

pointy face looking at a clipboard. 'Sadie Frost?' I nodded nervously and we were led into a huge hall with a floor as shiny as ice. All the other new girls seemed to have perfect teeth and perfect hair scraped back and glossed with lacquer. As I pulled my cape straight, I felt uncomfortable in my own skin. That morning I'd spent ages putting my hair in pigtails and left the house as neat as could be but suddenly everything about me seemed to be untidy.

'Where is Sadie Frost?' bellowed the teacher.

'I'm 'ere, miss,' I said loudly.

Some of the other girls sniggered. As they all answered their names I noticed how clearly and properly they spoke and I felt ashamed. As usual I was the odd one out. Wrong accent and uniform askew, I was the street urchin again. I bit back the tears and focused on the teacher. I wasn't going to let anyone ruin my dream. This was where I wanted to be: the shiny floors, the higgledy-piggledy old staircases and funny hidden rooms. There was a sense of order that I wanted and needed.

For all my wanting, I wasn't the model student. The other girls seemed more determined and talented than me. We would practise our arabesques and jetés at the bar in the grand hall and I could see how high they got their pink-stockinged legs and how tight their routines were. At break time girls would congregate in the corners of the hall with others of their age, opening their gym bags and pulling out snacks carefully made and packed by their mothers. The first years would all huddle together and do each other's

GROWING UP

hair, me and Rudi always sticking together. Another little group would split off from the rest; these were the four or five best pupils and although I knew I wasn't one of the best I still wanted to be in their gang. Amanda Mealing, Frances Ruffelle and Lisa Maxwell were the 'in crowd' and were busy gossiping and painting freckles on to each other's faces. Then we would all get down on the floor and start limbering up. I would sit on Rudi's legs while she stretched her muscles, then she would do the same for me. We wouldn't pause for breath while we did this, continuing to chat at full speed. After the break we would all line up for the teacher to look at us.

'Sadie Frost, what's happened to your leotard?' she said during one inspection.

I looked down and it seemed to be slipping off my shoulder and was all bunched round my bum. The other girls tittered.

'I ... um ... forgot to take my pants off, miss,' I said.

The teacher pointed to the changing room.

'Go and tidy yourself up, please, Sadie. This is the third time this week I've had to tell you.'

I took myself off disappointed; there was always something wrong with my outfit. Everything was so strict: jazz trousers and black pumps for modern dance, pink tights and pumps for ballet, and there was always something I'd left at home or forgotten to put on.

After school I would take the tube home and sometimes Mum and Frosty would meet me at Chalk Farm station.

They'd bring Sunny and Jessie and surprise me and we would all go to Marine Ices for a Knickerbocker Glory. Marine Ices was the best ice-cream parlour in the world and luckily it happened to be in Camden. It was painted in pretty pastel colours and inside there were steel benches to sit on, like in the American diners I would see in the movies. Those afternoons were full of laughter and we'd all get chocolate sauce on our faces after licking the bowl and then finishing it off with our fingers.

'Right, kids, who wants a bottle of pop and a packet of Hula Hoops?' said Frosty as he cleared away the ice cream one day. Not being content with the ice cream, me and Sunny put our hands up, as if in the classroom.

'So let's go to the beer garden then!' said Frosty, laughing, and gave Mum a peck on the cheek. That day, and many like it, we all walked up Haverstock Hill noisily talking over each other, reporting back on the day at school and stopping in at all the pubs, where the adults had a half of beer while we had a lemonade or a Coke. The first pub on the hill was the Load of Hay, next it was into the Sir Richard Steele and then we'd finish up at the Haverstock Arms, where Mum used to work part-time as a barmaid. She and Frosty would sit outside in the pub garden and smoke roll-ups but their adult talk would soon lose us and me, Sunny and Jessie would take our crisps and create an imaginary world in the corner. Once, a group of children were in the pub garden and they were staring at my Italia Conti uniform.

GROWING UP

'What are you dressed like that for?' said a little girl, looking slightly jealously at my cape and boater.

'No reason,' I replied.

'It's silly,' said a boy with her who was perhaps her brother.

I decided to ignore them and instead show off a few of my dance moves. For this I needed a stage and so I climbed on top of the wooden table in my full uniform and performed a tap routine.

'Wave your hands in the air like you just don't CARE!' I shouted at my audience below and at the same time I picked up my skirt and flashed my knickers. Sunny and Jessie fell on the floor laughing and the other children ran off in total shock.

'Get off that table, Sadie!' shouted Mum, noticing the commotion and shaking her head at me in mock horror.

Sometimes, though, I'd get home to Mum and Frosty and my sisters and it would feel glum or there would be an argument. I'd take off my uniform and put my school shirts out to wash. Unlike the others at Italia Conti, I didn't have the privilege of a whole wardrobe full of clothes to wear to school: I just had a couple of skirts and a jumper that Mum proudly ironed for me. Usually our flat was noisy and sometimes when I got back there would be a party going on and the place would be full of music and adults. But I clung on to my school life and so the rest didn't bother me too much. I would ignore everything and get on with my homework, making sure I was in bed early to get a good night's sleep. I could see

Mum smiling to herself as she stood over the ironing board getting the creases out of my crisp white shirt, as if she was pleased to see me turn from a grubby tomboy into a well-behaved daughter.

In bed I would retreat into my fantasy world and listen to Sunshine chattering away to her dolls in the bunk below. How could we be sisters and yet so different? She was blonde and gentle, I was dark and restless, constantly searching. I reached out and grabbed a rosary off my dressing table. It felt cold next to my flesh.

As I lay in bed and stared at the ceiling I saw blood dripping through the cracks in the wall, at first a little, then a lot, like a gently opening wound. I sat up and examined it more closely, aware that my whole body was shivering.

'Please, God, keep me safe and don't let me die,' I whispered, squeezing my eyes shut. When I finally opened them, the blood had gone but I was still clasping the beads. I scrambled off the bunk bed, wrote a note for my mum, then crept out and shoved it under her bedroom door. It said, 'I think I'm going to die.'

Lately it seemed that all I thought about was death. It was as if a black fuzz invaded my head every time I was happy, and suddenly I would imagine dying and not being here any more. It just seemed so awful that I was happy at school and yet there could be an end to it all. I couldn't sleep because of the worry, as well as the music and laughter blaring from the other room and the now familiar smell of what Frosty called 'dope'. I got up and fetched

GROWING UP

my favourite book, *Little Women*, and started to read, but every time I forgot about death and concentrated on the story, someone would get ill and nearly die. Eventually I fell asleep and in the morning I went to check the sitting room. Mum and Frosty were obviously asleep but everyone else had gone, leaving bottles and mess everywhere. I gathered all the glasses and plates and washed up, then cleaned all the surfaces with soap and a cloth. Finally I woke Sunshine and Jessie and made sure they had breakfast.

'Bloody, bloody hell,' said Sunny, dropping her spoon. I turned round, shocked that she was picking up bad habits from the adults, and grabbed the soap from the sink.

'Do not say that word. It's a sin and you'll go to hell when you die.'

'Bloody hell,' said Jessie, copying her.

I grabbed Jessie and put the soap in her mouth, resisting her struggling and spitting.

'You will wash your mouth out now!' I insisted, grabbing Sunny by the arm and forcing the soap into her mouth too. In my head things were clouded by death and sin. I wanted everything to be clean – the house, my sisters, our minds – so that nothing could get us.

'We have to be good girls!' I said as I dressed them afterwards. If I was a good girl, then I could keep us all together as a family. This need to look after and rescue didn't just stop at home. On the way to school I used to see a tramp who was always outside Belsize Park tube station and I would say hello to him every day. Sometimes I would even take him some food from home or from my packed lunch and sit and talk to him. I wasn't scared at all; in fact I felt attracted to people that other kids would stay away from. Once, me and Rudi had taken a detour across Clapham Common on our way to school and I dropped down to do up my shoe. From the bushes nearby I heard a rustle and went to have a look.

'Sadie! Come *ooon*. We'll be late again,' whined Rudi, walking ahead.

'I'll catch you up,' I said, my curiosity taking over. In the bushes there was a man, wearing a brown coat and dirty jeans, who seemed to be busy doing something inside his coat. He urged me to go closer but at the last minute something made me stop. At the same time he opened his coat. Even now I couldn't understand what he was doing, rubbing something pink between his hands. Then I realised, and turned and ran.

'Rudi! Rudi! Wait!' I shouted.

'What is it?' she said as I caught up with her, panting as I corrected my cape and boater and pulled up my white knee socks.

'Nothing,' I said, walking on in silence. Soon afterwards it happened again, but this time it was a different man. It appeared that Clapham Common was a place where men liked to show me their penises. I wondered about this, because they didn't seem to do it to other girls and it always happened when I was in my school uniform. What was this effect that I had on men? It made me uncomfortable but at the same time it intrigued me.

Things that other kids stayed away from seemed to pull me in. After school I would get changed and go to the flat next door to see my friend Sylvia. Eighty years old, she had a beard and cataracts in her eyes. Most people didn't talk to Sylvia, who lived with another old lady, but I was always in there, talking to them about my life, helping them pin their big, off-white knickers on the line. I was worried that Sylvia would die soon, or worried that no one would take care of her if she needed help.

My concern for old people and the tramp who lived at the tube station almost took over, and I would go to risky houses in the area, looking for the tramp and his friends. I got to know where they squatted and I'd happily take them food. I was the same with animals, always rescuing an injured bird or a mouse. Once I found a little chick with a broken wing and took it to my room to nurse. But there was something inside me that liked the sense that I might be doing something dangerous. It was a battle inside me, between the good girl and the bad one, that was to do with my father. He was like a poison in me and I could feel him trying to rise up and engulf the tidy, clean part. I wanted order but I also wanted danger. Sometimes the need for danger would get the better of me. I would lead my friends into derelict buildings or get them to play on wasteland that often contained big holes or jagged glass. This excited me and made me popular with the local boys.

'Want to come to my house for tea?' said Mark, a boy that I coaxed into one particularly unstable building. I shrugged, but that meant yes. He lived in a big house round the corner from my flat in Haverstock Hill but I wasn't impressed, remembering my father's attitude to the rich. His mother smiled as she put the brown soup down in front of me. It smelled suspiciously like meat.

'I'm not eating this, I'm a vegetarian,' I said quickly. Mark's mother looked shocked and then tried to smile again.

'It's not really meat,' she said. 'It's oxtail. So eat it up. It's rude not to.'

I crossed my arms and lifted my chin. 'I will not eat it,' I said, staring at her defiantly.

'You will do as you are told,' she shot back.

'Make me then,' I said, getting up from the table. The look of shock on Mark's face was amazing. Children didn't argue with other people's mothers, but I didn't care. I liked the confrontation and the attention it brought. It was as if my dad were there with me. I didn't see the lady's hand coming as it clipped me round the ear and stung, but I looked at her with a triumphant smile and ran to the front door. It wasn't the first or the last time I'd get hit. By now I was quite used to it and I wasn't going to stop arguing back.

The summer holiday away from Italia Conti was the only time I got to go and see my dad. I would swap my starched uniform for a pair of high-waisted pink flares and take the

GROWING UP

train to Manchester, enjoying the anticipation of the journey as much as I'd always enjoyed going back there to the safety of my grandparents' house in Denton. This time my Dad and his new wife Anne were waiting to meet me off the train at Stockport.

Anne and Dad had two children together, Simon and Jamie, and there was a new baby, called Toby. I'd first met Anne a few years before, when I was seven and Mum had taken me and Sunny up to Denton for a holiday. Anne had taken us to see her horse, Albert, and I'd hardly spoken to her all day, even when I had a ride on him. Sunny was chatting away with her happily but I wouldn't. It was because she wasn't my mum but I was already in love with my little half-brothers, who were all angelic-looking with long, curly hair.

As I got off the train this time, now 11 years old, I didn't feel any more like being nice to her even though she went out of her way to be nice to me. I liked being Daddy's girl and I didn't want anyone else around. I flew into my dad's arms, breathing in deep his familiar smoky smell.

'Eee up. Bloody hell, you've grown, lass,' he said cheerfully. 'How's my bloody beautiful actress then?'

We caught up on all my school news as he drove me to work with him in Hulme, a rough part of Manchester where he was a youth worker. He had a painting business called The Ark that painted murals in deprived areas. Everywhere he went, the kids crowded round him and looked on him as a hero. He would get everyone, including me, painting a mural on a wall and adopt local youths who wanted to be rock musicians or artists. There would always be a couple of lads hanging round him with a guitar, their impossibly wide flares fluttering in the wind.

Dad would introduce me to them and I could see them looking me up and down.

'This is my prodigy daughter from London,' he would tell them with a warning look in his eyes that said, 'Touch her and you are dead.'

'I wanna be the next Mark Bolan,' they would tell my dad, who would grin and nod to their guitar and say, 'You need to bloody learn to play the bloody thing first.' I was part of Dad's new life but also not part of it and that bothered me. I ignored his relationship with Anne, thinking that it wouldn't last long. No one's relationships seemed to last long, or if they did, they were full of rows and violence.

One day Dad took me for a drive and a chat, pointing out sights as we drove along. 'That's the swings that I first went to with your brothers Tim and Daniel.'

'I haven't got any brothers called Tim or Daniel,' I replied, laughing. But Dad just went quiet, before saying, 'Yes you have. They live here in Manchester. From my first wife, before your mum.'

We passed the rest of the drive in silence. I couldn't believe that I had yet more brothers and that neither my dad nor my mum had told me. All of a sudden I was filled with curiosity and desperate to meet them. I had always

GROWING UP

been the oldest but suddenly I realised that not only did I have older teenage brothers but that, although related to me, they were *boys* – boys I was allowed to associate with. I made it my mission to find them but Dad wasn't at all helpful as I nagged away at him.

'I don't bloody know where they are, Sadie. They could be anywhere. Manchester is a big place and I don't talk to their mam.'

Eventually, by asking everyone I could in the whole of Denton, I got a phone number for Dad's ex-wife. I called it and held my breath.

'Hello? Who is that?' I said in my poshest voice.

'Tim,' said a grumpy male voice. 'Who's askin'?'

'It's Sadie... I'm your sister,' I said, almost drowning in excitement.

Tim and I arranged to meet and Dad said it was OK for us to go for a walk in the Pennines above Ashton together. It was the first time I'd ever been alone for a long time with a boy. Tim told me that Daniel wasn't around and he wouldn't tell me where he was, so I had to make do with knowing only him. As far as I was concerned, having an older brother made me feel special, and I was a little bit in love with Tim.

Dad could sense this and acted like a kid in an effort to get my attention back. For his first little joke he spiced up my vegetarian casserole with so much chilli powder that I had to run to the sink and wash my mouth out. Then he'd sneak into my room in the middle of the night and whisper, 'Get dressed, we're going for a drive,' and I'd get into his van bleary-eyed and we'd drive out to some estate where he'd be painting a wall in a rainbow of colours. At the same time, as good as he could be when he wasn't drinking too much, he was still Vaughany, jealous and liable to turn into a madman. One time when he was arguing with Anne, Jamie and Simon were crying and the three of us huddled together with me trying to protect them from him as they shouted at him to stop throwing things. Dad picked up Jamie and tried to chuck him out of the window.

'Dad, stop, please,' I screamed and held on to Jamie until he relented and the child hugged me for dear life. I should have been more scared than I was, but Dad made me feel so special that even his rage meant attention to me, and suffering his temper seemed to be worth it.

It was with relief that I got back on the train to London, but I was to find unsettling scenes at home, too. Mum and Frosty's relationship was breaking down and some of their rows became violent. With Sunny and Jessie crying, I got dressed in the middle of the night and ran to the local police station in Belsize Park, arriving breathless at the front desk.

'Can you come quick!' I panted to the duty officer. 'My mum and stepdad are fighting.' Soon after, Mum announced that Frosty was moving out. Me and my sisters watched him leave and cried. I'd been a bad stepdaughter, often liking to disagree with him just because I could, but all the same I still loved him. Yet in a way it meant the end of the rows and I convinced myself this was a good thing.

As life was changing around me once more, I noticed that my body was changing and odd things were starting to happen, like sprouting breasts. My friends and I were taking more interest in boys. I was nearly 12 years old and starting to feel uneasy in my own skin.

Then Mum introduced us to her new boyfriend. 'This is Robert,' she said, looking tenderly at the strange man in the sitting room. He was cross-legged and had very long hair, which wasn't surprising because all Mum's male friends had long hair and beards, but Robert was different because his skin was almost orange and he was dressed from head to foot in purple clothes. The house was suddenly filled with crystals and Robert had a black box with knobs on it that turned out to be central to the healing he practised. A lot of the decisions at home were made by Robert swinging a pendulum.

'Robert is going to come and live with us,' Mum explained, as her new man lit a special candle. 'He's a follower of Bhagwan Rajneesh.'

'What?' I said, confused and a little put out.

'He's a healer. He heals by colour, and the healing colour is purple. He belongs to the Bhagwan faith.'

I rolled my eyes and left the room. It was time for school, so I gladly put on my cape and boater and took off. Now there was a new man in our life, Italia Conti was even more welcome. At first it made me more determined to succeed there. I took extra singing and tap lessons and got myself in with Amanda Mealing and Frances Ruffelle, all the time trying extra hard to make the top of the class. Every morning a list of names would be pinned to the notice board. Sometimes it would say: 'COULD S. FROST, F. RUFFELLE, A. MEALING COME TO THE OFFICE TO ATTEND AN AUDITION?'

If my name was on that list, it made my day, but if I wasn't, the day was ruined. Along with Bonnie Langford, me and Frances and Amanda formed a dance group that became successful at Conti and we were chosen to dance at the Royal Festival Hall. I would force myself forward into the spotlight even though my shyness meant that auditions terrified me so much that I would be sick. Eventually I was chosen to star in a television film about a girl's friendship with a talking horse. For me, filming was a shocking thing. I was stunned at the number of people on the set, and as I was taken there I froze like a rabbit caught in headlights. There were too many people and too much going on. Even the catering table seemed like it was buckling under the weight. I'd never seen so much food.

When I got home, bursting with news about my film debut despite my fears, Mum and Robert were busy packing. 'We're getting a new place,' said Mum excitedly. 'It's great, not damp, so your chest will be better, and you'll have a garden to get plenty of fresh air. So get packing!'

I had now accepted that Robert was not going anywhere

GROWING UP

and I'd have to put up with him. I'd heard him talking to Mum earlier about his plans.

'The Bhagwan's followers have taken over the Roundhouse, man,' he said, slowly wafting a candle about the room and waving his hands. 'The future is all gonna be about us now, the Bhagwan faith,' he said, smiling, then kissed my mum. As usual, I refused to believe that anything good would come out of their relationship and that soon it would go the way of my dad and Frosty.

But 11 Lyndhurst Gardens was a nicer flat, even though it was in the basement and had no windows. I now had my own room, which was much bigger and again I turned it into a boudoir, decorating it with old perfume bottles. I also decided that I wanted a proper bed off the floor. I found some dismantled scaffolding on a nearby building site and took it home, erecting a sort of bed frame that raised the mattress up. Soon the flat was completely purple, like Robert, and soon Mum started wearing purple too. I was made to lie down in the new sitting room while Robert carried out a healing ceremony on my damaged lung.

'Lie still, Sadie,' he said as he plucked a hair from my head and put it in his special machine, which was surrounded by candles.

'How's that gonna heal my lung, then?' I said, doubting everything that was going on.

'Patience, darling,' said Robert, fiddling with the machine. 'From now on you don't eat any dairy products and your lung will improve.' I tutted and got up. I was fed up with the Bhagwan thing and thought it was all stupid. It didn't fit in with my school and my ambitions. The changes at home and the changes in my body couldn't help but affect my attitude to school. Conti had been my whole existence but now things were less clear-cut. The discipline it demanded was starting to annoy me and the part of me that was the Good Sadie was listening to the whispering of my developing body, which seemed to say, 'Change... change...', like the gentle rustling of leaves in the wind.

CHAPTER FOUR

That Boy

I opened my eyes and watched the rain through the bay window. Through the drops of water I saw him: his blond hair choppy and spiked, his cheekbones as perfect as a china doll, his eyes ice blue. He smoked and laughed at the same time, moving easily inside his tartan drainpipe trousers and studded leather jacket. I was aware of my breath on the back of my hand which was touching the glass of the window. The window that I was behind, standing in my smart uniform. I was alone in my ivory tower. This is how I felt. I was in my glass bubble inside the bay window and he was outside my world, the world that existed when I was in the blue cape and straw boater. I want that boy... I want to marry that boy...

I opened my eyes once more and stared at my reflection in the window pane, my shiny plaited hair and Italia Conti smile. Something made me lean forward and breathe on it, steam it up, the way I did when I was very young. It was a way to block out my face and block out who I was.

'Are you paying attention, Sadie?' said the teacher loudly.

'Yes, miss, sorry, miss,' I said, snapping my gaze back to the classroom. The other pupils looked up from their books and wrinkled their brows at me, wondering what I'd done this time. Every two minutes it seemed as if one or other of the teachers was on my back. As soon as she turned around to the blackboard to write up some more French words that I didn't understand, I turned to the window again. Three girls wandered along the street below, listening to a tape recorder and wearing ripped jeans and denim jackets with studs all over them. I refocused on my reflection in the glass, sending the girls into a blur.

'Comment tu t'appelles?' barked the teacher again, noticing me staring once more out of the window.

'Sorry, miss, yes, miss. Je m'appelle … je m'appelle…'

Sunshine had recently been coming home from her comprehensive school with a new style, a style that I didn't have. The previous day she'd returned with her hair cut short and jagged and although she was a couple of years younger than me, suddenly she seemed much older. She looked tougher, like she might know about stuff that I should know about. Music and parties and stuff that teenagers were into. The worst thing was that the blond boy with the ice-blue eyes, *my* boy, even said hello to her when she passed.

THAT BOY

'Who is that boy?' I asked Sunny as she came through the door and dropped her school bag.

'He's called Lucien,' she said off-handedly.

'How come he talked to you?' I pressed as she went to the kitchen to make toast.

'He goes to my school, stupid,' she said, trying her best to ignore me.

We had moved house again with Bhagwan Robert, but this time not into a basement. We'd managed to get a first-floor flat in Gondar Gardens, West Hampstead. It was a light, sunny flat arranged over two floors and Mum worked hard to make it a home. We had new furniture, including a beige corner sofa that was her pride and joy. Robert was a gentle man and apparently a pacifist. I sensed Mum needed some stability around the place, and Robert gave her that, with his hippy healing and his gardening. They had got married in Scotland and now she was pregnant with his baby. The bad thing about Gondar Gardens was that Dad wasn't around.

Despite my dad's chaos, no other man was good enough for my mum, or for our family. The good thing about Gondar Gardens, however, was Lucien. The love of my life even though he didn't yet know it.

I brought my thoughts back to the classroom and the present. The teacher was staring at me with rising irritation.

'Sadie! Je m'appelle *who*?' she said. 'Don't you know who you are?'

I was saved from answering that question by the bell

signalling the end of the lesson, and I packed up my things, then headed to the lunch room. Rudi fell into step next to me.

'Are you OK?' she said, staring at me doubtfully, seeing that I was far away.

'Yeah.'

'Guess what we've got for lunch,' she said, smiling. 'Angel Delight.'

I forgot about my sister and Lucien for a minute and returned Rudi's smile. Angel Delight was a favourite and a craze sweeping the school. I loved the way it just came from a bit of powder into this pink, fluffy, sweet-tasting custard that left a strange fur coating on the inside of your mouth. We took extra helpings of it and smuggled it out of the dining hall, dashing to the changing room to get ready for ballet. For some reason, something possessed me to put my fingers in the pink, sticky goo and flick it at Rudi. After her initial shock, she did the same to me, and I replied by pelting her with a huge scoop that hit a mirror behind her. Another couple of girls also got hit by the stuff and joined in, scooping more out of the bowl and lobbing it at Rudi. I wiped the mess off the mirror and stared at my long black hair. It was as if there was a force inside me urging me on.

'Rudi, give me your scissors.'

Rudi stopped for a second and looked at me. 'Why. What are you going to do?'

'Just give them to me.'

Rudi brought me the little scissors that she kept in her

pencil case and I grabbed a wedge of my hair and cut it into a short, jagged fringe. Rudi and the others froze, unable to move an inch as I stared at my new hairstyle with a mixture of pride and fear.

'*Sadie Frost! What are you doing?*'

I turned around slowly. Mrs Mellon was standing with her hands on her hips at the entrance of the changing room. She moved her eyes between each of the other girls, now covered in Angel Delight, then to me – not only pink and sticky, but also looking like a scarecrow with a ragged fringe.

'You are in a good deal of trouble, young lady,' she said, before turning me round and marching me off to the headmistress's office, where I was made to wait while Mrs Mellon got a camera and took a Polaroid of my chopped fringe.

'That is for your mother,' she said curtly as she got her coat on to take me to the nearest hairdressers to have my hair cut back into a normal shape. I felt a deep sense of shame, not wanting to get into trouble. Conti was my life, my bubble, and I needed it. When we got back to school my mother was waiting for me, having been told about the Angel Delight incident.

'What do you think you're playing at, Sadie?' she whispered angrily as we took the tube home.

'Sorry,' I said, hanging my head.

'Is that all you can say? Sorry? You've coated the school in bloody Angel Delight and cut your hair like a punk rocker. I'm in shock, Sadie. This is what you wanted, this is your dream – remember?'

We spent the rest of the journey in silence, and the whole of that evening. In the end I could stand it no more and begged to be allowed to go over to Rudi's to play. Tired of my pestering, Mum finally agreed. Rudi's house was in Mornington Crescent, not far from Camden Town, and it was amazing. Her mother was a famous author called Beryl Bainbridge who was very eccentric in her tastes. It wasn't like anyone else's house and I loved going there because there was always something exotic that I didn't know about. In the entrance hall there was a real stuffed buffalo and instead of a normal phone they had one of those old red phone boxes.

Rudi and I sat in her bedroom, full up after a delicious dinner. Her mother had given me an avocado salad with something called French dressing, which was new to me and tasted wonderful. Rudi put on a David Bowie album, stolen from her sister's collection, and we started fiddling with our hair and doing our make-up while we sang along: 'Will you stay in my lovers' story…'

Rudi had bright red hair and freckles and was adding some turquoise eye shadow that clashed with everything.

'What are you doing?' she said, watching me put dark purple eye shadow all over my cheeks.

'This is how the punks put it on,' I said, checking out the effect in the mirror.

'I'm going to see my sister at the weekend,' said Rudi,

trying to outdo me. 'Mum is letting me get the train all on my own to Liverpool.'

'So?' I said, trying to pretend that I didn't care that she had the freedom and excitement in her life that I wanted.

'And guess what else,' she said, not satisfied with my response. 'I'm leaving Italia Conti.'

This time I dropped the make-up brush and stared at her full in the face, her elfin little face with white skin that looked like it didn't quite fit. Rudi was my best friend at Conti and the prospect of being there without her was something I didn't even want to think about. My expression must have said it all.

'Why?'

Rudi shrugged. 'Mum said if I don't want to stay there I don't have to.'

I walked home with feet like lead, not looking up from the pavement once. It was as if my world was falling in, piece by piece. All I wanted to do was run away from everything I knew.

On Saturday morning I got up, packed a bag and headed down to King's Cross. I'd arranged to meet up with Rudi at 10am to get the train to Liverpool. She was early, I was late, running to meet her at the platform.

'I thought you weren't coming,' she said breathlessly as we boarded the train. 'I thought your mum had said you weren't allowed to come.'

'Course I'm allowed,' I lied, smiling at her as we sat opposite each other at a table next to the window. We giggled all the way to Liverpool, planning what we were going to do and which clubs we would try to get into. As the countryside flew by, I felt different, like I didn't care about anything any more apart from being free to do what I wanted. When we got to Lime Street station, Rudi searched the crowd for a glimpse of her sister.

'There she is!' she said, running towards a tall woman in a black coat. I lagged behind, hoping Rudi would do all the explaining for me, about how I'd left home and wanted to get a place to live. As I joined them, I knew that Rudi's sister's eyes spelled trouble.

'Are you Sadie?' she said, looking at me suspiciously.

'Yeah,' I said, chewing gum and swinging my bag, trying desperately to look confident. 'I'm going to live on the streets.'

'Right, well, your mum rang me and told me that you'd run away and that I'm to put you on the first train back to London. She'll meet you at King's Cross.'

Rudi looked away, suddenly not wanting to get involved, and my head dropped again. I hated my mother for getting in the way, hated the world for humiliating me in front of Rudi's sister. As far as I was concerned, Rudi had won and I had lost. She was leaving and I was being left behind.

Back at King's Cross a few hours later, I was met by Mum and Robert, who looked at me as if I'd disappointed them for ever.

'Sorry,' I said as we got into Robert's car.

'Is that all you can say? Sorry?' said Robert. 'You had us worried to death. What were you playing at?'

'Running away.'

'What the hell do you want to run away for?' said Mum, twisting round to face me in the back seat. I folded my arms across my chest and looked straight out of the window, refusing to answer. 'You're throwing it all away by behaving like this. You got a scholarship to stage school and the way you're behaving you'll muck it up.'

But all of a sudden I didn't care about acting or dancing or appearing in television films. It was never really about being an actress, it was about being at Italia Conti, that was what I'd wanted. I'd needed it to make me stand out. As the posh girl with a smart uniform I'd felt safe from harm and from the chaos at home. But now all I wanted was danger. I wanted boys and love and kissing and the smells of teenagers, pot, hair dye, make-up, leather, studs, punk rock, records, cigarettes, music, fights and trouble. 'I don't care. I'm leaving Italia Conti.'

'You are not,' said Mum in a deeper, worried voice.

'I am,' I said, looking her dead in the eye. 'I hate it there and I'm never going back and you can't make me.'

A week later I'd thrown away my uniform and was now wearing a non-uniform luminous mohair jumper and stripy socks as I stepped nervously through the gates of Hampstead Comprehensive. For once I was letting Sunshine lead the way. It made me feel awkward that she should have the upper hand and I refused to let my nervousness show as she took me round the school. As we walked past the drama block, I saw a gang of kids dressed in leather jackets and tight jeans huddled together, a plume of smoke escaping from between them.

'What's going on?' I whispered to Sunny as we passed the group.

'That's where the smokers hang out,' she said knowledgeably.

As we passed I stole another look at the group of boys and my heart leapt into my mouth when I saw him: Lucien, the blond, beautiful boy. The boy that a few weeks before I had sworn to myself that I would marry. He looked up as we passed, exhaling smoke into the cold air, hollowing his perfect cheekbones even more. It was as if he held all my hopes and dreams, and he didn't even know the power he already had over me.

Sunny left me at my new form room and the nervousness returned. The teacher, a tired-looking man in a crumpled suit, came in and started cleaning the blackboard. No one seemed to take any notice of him, apart from me, who was used to sitting rod-straight and silent as soon as a teacher entered the room. Some of the boys were chewing gum and flicking each other with pencils, but most of the class seemed to be looking at me and wondering who I was.

'OK, you horrible lot, please can you open your textbooks and do the work on the board.'

Everyone opened their books, reluctantly starting to work,

but I didn't have a book and the maths on the board looked impossibly complicated. I put my hand up and eventually got the teacher's attention. 'Please, sir, I don't have a textbook,' I said in the most confident voice I could manage. I wasn't prepared for the response from my classmates, who all began laughing at me.

'Ooh, get her, all la-di-da posh,' said one of the boys.

'That's enough,' said the teacher, calling me to up his desk. But it was too late. I'd gone bright red and wanted the floor to open up. To the other kids I was the posh girl from private school, who had been having elocution lessons for the last five years. At break time I went and sat alone, heartbroken that my old dream had made my new dream more impossible. I wanted to blend in with these cool kids but instead my stage-school education had made me the odd one out. All day the kids teased me about my accent, making me talk so that they could mimic my posh voice.

That night I cried myself to sleep, feeling the damp patch on the pillow spread. Wasn't there anywhere I could just be me? At Italia Conti I'd been the poor scholarship girl and now I was the posh kid. It didn't seem fair. In the morning I forced myself out of bed and decided to do something about it. My long, black, perfect bob, which had been my pride and joy, was coming off. I got the scissors and finished what I had started at Conti, shearing it all off until I'd achieved the cropped punk look that the cool lads at school had. To top it off I grabbed one of Sunny's music magazines and copied the make-up of one of the punk bands. As I dashed out of the door, eager to avoid Mum and Bobby, as we all called him now, I ran straight into them. Mum looked at me in shock and Bobby just shook his head sadly.

'What?' I said, looking daggers at my stepfather, who just went on into the house. I wasn't in the mood for his opinion, and as far as I was concerned he had no right even to be in our house, or lives. Mum blocked my path, wanting to talk. She could see that I was angry and confused and she wanted to help, probably longing to hug me and shower me with her unconditional love, but I just barged past her. I didn't really care if she was hurting because I was being so horrible, or care that she was pregnant and throwing herself into her new life with Bobby. It was as if she always needed a strong man to give her strength. But all that meant to me was that I'd seen a lot of rows and physical fights, with my dad, then Frosty. I took all this anger and rolled it up into a ball. Inside, wound tightly like the inside of a golf ball, I was a mass of rage. In the back of my mind I didn't want to think about the guilt I felt about quitting stage school because now I was on Mission Lucien, and nothing was going to get in my way.

The trouble was that I had a lot of catching up to do and set about doing it. The first weekend after starting at my new school I went down to Kensington Indoor Market, where all the punks went, and bought myself a leopard-

THAT BOY

skin coat and a pair of Dr Martens. Next it was the chemist for the red hair dye. Back at home, I locked myself away in my room and set about making myself into a punk. It worked because at school on Monday morning a girl came up to me and shoved me in the arm.

'You're that new posh girl, aren't you?' she said pulling her gum out of her mouth.

'I ain't posh,' I said, trying desperately to rough up my plummy voice.

'Well, I don't care if you are,' she said, spinning the chewing gum round her finger to make a ring. 'I like your hair. I'm Beth Cinamon. You wanna come and smoke behind the drama block?' she asked, popping the gum back in her mouth and not waiting for me to reply before she took off. Beth was by far the coolest girl I'd ever seen. Her hair was shaved down the middle and gelled up in the shape of cat's ears on either side. I discovered that the punks hung out behind the drama block and Beth introduced me to the girl with the cigarettes, Sarah Dove, and the three of us fell into chatting about the latest Spizz Energy record. I wasn't that sure what Spizz Energy sounded like but I made a mental note to swot up on all punk music that evening. I took the cigarette from Sarah and breathed it in deeply, desperate not to choke. As I exhaled I hoped that none of the others would notice me going green with nausea. I never smoked because of my bad lung, but to hell with that.

'Here get a sniff of this, love,' said one of the boys as he unscrewed a bottle of Tippex correction fluid, poured it on to the cuff of his denim jacket and thrust it into my face.

'Go on, it gets you high,' said Beth, clearly amused as she watched me. If this was a test I wasn't going to fail it now. I took a deep breath, feeling the chemicals rush in with it, making their way round my already overloaded brain. Suddenly I was in with the punks and smoking and sniffing Tippex. Could things get any better? As the dizziness cleared I realised that the gathering was breaking up because the bell had rung for the next lesson. Standing there was Lucien, looking at me through the crowd. For a split second I smiled but at that very moment a girl stood in my way and his attention was lost. I went to my next class wondering when and how I could see him again. The answer was obvious: I knew where he lived, right opposite me, so all I had to do was follow him home from school. Later that afternoon I waited by the school gate until he and his older brother Devlin came out. As Lucien passed, kicking a stone and smoking, I smiled, but he looked straight through me, as though I was a ghost, like I wasn't there. Gutted, I followed along behind, trying to keep a suitable distance, and loitered around while they went into the corner shop. I took out my compact mirror and checked my make-up, my white face a contrast with my red hair and dark lipstick. I knew that boys liked the look of me, and although I hadn't kissed a boy for three years, I wasn't scared of them. But Lucien seemed to be on another level. In my eyes he wasn't a boy, he was a God. A perfect human specimen.

THAT BOY

The next weekend Beth asked me to come out with her and I agreed excitedly. As I was getting ready, to my delight Dad called and Mum shouted to me that he was on the phone.

'Eee up, princess,' he said. 'How's my darling girl?'

'Brilliant, Dad, but I haven't got time to talk 'cos I'm going to a party,' I said breathlessly.

'Eee, a bloody party, eh? Get you. Where?' he replied, sounding a bit upset that I didn't have time to talk.

'At the Music Machine. You have to be over 17 to get in but we're going anyway.' The Music Machine was the latest name for the old Camden Palace and it was where all the punk bands of the day played, including the chart-toppers Adam and the Ants. Beth and Sarah came to pick me up to go to the club. Sarah had a mass of back-combed hair and a pair of tartan bondage trousers and Beth was wearing black lipstick. Sarah was the best dressed of the three of us. She modelled herself on the girl punk group the Slits and her parents were fashion designers who printed punk T-shirts in a warehouse in Dollis Hill and had a shop called BOY on the King's Road. As I walked along with my two new friends, arms linked, I breathed the air in deeply and felt invincible.

After the Music Machine we met up with some of the boys from school, including Danny Pressman, Phil Rose and Rob Sable. We all went to hang out at the bus shelter in Golders Green and then on to a party. One boy had a plastic bag in his hands, gathered up like a balloon and with some stuff inside it, and every so often he would put his mouth and nose to the bag and breathe in deeply.

'What's that?' I said casually as he leaned back with his eyes closed after inhaling.

'Glue. Want a sniff?' he said, finally opening his eyes.

'No thanks.'

'Go on,' said another lad. He had been watching me and kept trying to kiss me, then suddenly he grabbed the bag and gave it to me. Immediately I felt anxiety but with the whole gang looking at me, and my place in it not yet secure, I closed my eyes and brought the bag to my mouth. Stars danced and swirled and my legs turned to jelly. I heard voices and laughter. All I knew was that I was laughing too, before the effect wore off, leaving me with a banging headache.

When we got to the party it seemed that half the school was there, including Lucien, who ignored me.

'Hi, Lucien,' I said pushing past a group of girls to reach him in the kitchen.

'Oh, er, hi,' he said, looking at me as if I was a little fly on his shoulder.

'You know me, I'm Sunshine's sister.' I cursed myself immediately for describing myself this way but had to do something to make him recognise me. He sort of laughed and made a face, as if I was a little kid who was annoying him. All the girls at school wanted him but I wanted him more.

At that moment an older girl came and snogged him and

I turned away, disappointed. Thing was, I knew that we'd be perfect together, and my fantasy had him centre stage.

Later that night, when it was time to get home, Danny, Phil, Beth and me found ourselves without money in the middle of nowhere. I had no option but to call Bobby and ask him to come and pick us up. After waiting for an hour we spotted his bright green VW camper van and gratefully crawled into the back.

'Thanks,' I said grudgingly, and Bobby smiled tiredly. 'No problem, dudes,' he said and I felt guilty for being so horrible to him most of the time, but he wasn't my dad.

'He's really cool,' whispered Danny to me as we rode alone. 'Can we come and hang out at your house?'

That night they all slept on my floor and the next morning Mum made them a vegetarian breakfast. They were impressed at how laid-back she was and my house instantly became *the* hang-out pad. There the boys were allowed to smoke their joints out of the window and not fear getting grounded. But if my flat was going to be the new hang-out place I had to get rid of all my girly boudoir decorations and do something radical. I called my dad, as just the man for the job, and asked him if he would come down to London and help me graffiti my bedroom walls. He jumped at the chance but as soon as he arrived I regretted it. It had been a while since I'd seen him and he was just as demanding of my attention as ever. But the thing was, he was a brilliant painter and my bedroom soon looked like a proper piece of graffiti art.

'Wow, that is wicked,' said Danny as he jumped on my bed and sparked up a joint. My dad sat on the bed next to him and took the joint out of his hand, toking on it himself.

'So where's the party tonight then, Sadie?' said Dad, settling in. Danny looked as uncomfortable as I felt and I grabbed my jacket and made eyes to Danny to move out.

'Oh, it's, erm, miles away.'

'Bloody great,' he continued, rubbing his hands in anticipation. 'Let's go.'

'It's teenagers, not grown men, Dad. I wanted you to paint my bedroom, not hang out with me.' My sharp tongue had obviously stung him because he recoiled instantly at the rejection. He looked down like a scolded child.

'It's final. You're not coming with us,' I added, fearing his response and not wanting him to fly off the handle in front of my mates. He didn't want to let me out of his sight, and even though Mum and Bobby were in the next room, I was scared he would kick off, so I gave him a quick kiss and rushed out of the door.

Lucien was in a band called the Paradox and me and Beth went to all their gigs and even their band practices in their bedrooms, which smelled of crude aftershave and sweat and were decorated with punk posters and had empty cans everywhere. After a while Lucien started to recognise me. At first he would laugh and shake his head when I turned up again and again, but soon he started to talk to me, realising that I was determined to be in his life.

THAT BOY

One night a group of us were at a party quite a way from London after watching the Paradox play a gig at a minor university. As usual I was the one who called my stepfather for a lift.

'Can you come and pick us up? We've got no money,' I whined down the phone.

'Um, yeah, um, OK,' said Bobby, sounding a bit strange. I didn't think any more about it until he pulled up next to the bus shelter where we were waiting.

'I have to be quick,' said Bobby as we piled into the camper van. 'Your mum has gone into labour at home.'

I was struck by guilt and fell silent. Bobby had driven miles to pick us up on the night that Mum was having his baby. I hadn't even considered what they were going through when I'd called. All that mattered was *me* getting a lift. When we got back Mum was having the baby in her bedroom. I felt sick and went out to sleep in the van. As far as I was concerned she was selfish and inconsiderate to do such a revolting thing as give birth in *my house*. But when I crept back indoors the next morning I found Mum holding the cutest baby I'd ever seen, with long eyelashes and eyebrows that looked like a caterpillar. Holly Emerald had big green eyes and a tiny, turned-up nose. Mum and Bobby were perfectly happy now their daughter had arrived.

As the school broke up for the summer, I begged Dad to take me away with him. He and Anne had saved up for ages to afford a trip to France, so I went on holiday with

Dad's new family. But it was as if I was a spare, because now that Dad and Mum both had new partners and kids, I didn't really fit in anywhere. Even though I was glad to be on holiday I'd rather have been having a summer of love with Lucien.

We arrived at the caravan park in France in high spirits. Dad was behaving well and hadn't been drinking too much on the journey and I made a special effort to be kind to Anne, who, I was discovering, was a very lovely woman. The caravan site was on the beach and the holiday started well, with all of us playing in the white fluffy sand and eating ice creams. Later I lay out on the beach, all skinny in my bikini, and watched the other teenagers, especially the boys, playing volleyball and having fun.

After a few days Dad got bored and started drinking Pernod. The caravan was tiny, not a place to start an argument, but I got angry with him because Anne was trying to put the boys to bed and he was lurching around destroying the place.

'God, Dad! You're so drunk. Why don't you just get out!' I shouted at him as he lurched through the little door and fell on my bed.

'Don't tell me to get out! It's my fuckin' caravan.'

'Why do you have to do this, Dave?' Anne screamed, tears running down her cheeks. 'Why do you have to ruin everything all the time?'

Dad grabbed a bottle and threw it at her, narrowly missing her but breaking the window.

THAT BOY

I grabbed the boys and we huddled together at one end of the caravan while he raged at Anne, grabbing her by her hair and hurling another bottle. I knew that I had to do something but was scared to leave the boys.

'Don't move from here,' I told them, looking at the fear in their faces. 'I'll be back in a second, OK?' I ran out of the door, wearing only my underwear and no shoes. No one was awake in the other caravans, so I went to bang on the door of the campsite reception. Finally the manager opened it.

'Oui?'

'P-p-please…' I stuttered, shaking with fear as I pointed to our caravan. 'You have to come and help. My dad is attacking his wife.'

At first he looked at my underwear as if I was a trophy and I felt very vulnerable under his gaze, so I repeated my plea in stuttering French, eventually making him understand I needed help. He grabbed a torch and a can of something and followed me. We could hear the screams coming from the caravan and the manager banged on the door with his torch. When Dad appeared at the door the manager sprayed Mace into his face. Dad gripped his head and flailed around, screaming in agony. I remained frozen to the spot. Suddenly the lights were on in every caravan and people came out to see what was going on. Guilt flooded over me as I watched my dad writhe about on the floor of the caravan. It was all my fault.

The next morning Dad shook me awake at 6am. He was fully dressed, with even his overcoat on.

'Get up and wake the boys, get 'em dressed and walk them down the beach.'

'Why?' I said, struggling to make sense of anything.

'Because we're doing a bloody runner, that's why. I'm skint,' he said.

I did as I was told and dressed the sleepy boys, all of us shivering as we stole out into the half light. We met up with Dad and Anne, who had brought the car to the beach. Nothing ever changed with Dad, and my heart sank as we ran away, like rats scurrying down a sewer. That's how being with him made me feel sometimes and it was his drinking that did it. All I wanted to do was get home to Hampstead and return to school and Lucien.

Back at school to start my O-level year, I worked hard – despite my obsession with Lucien and my new friends – to catch up on my work. At Conti there had been limited academic work and now I suddenly found myself about a year behind the others. But I didn't want to be the school dummy and always managed to find time to fit my homework in. It wasn't long before my Lucien worship turned into something more. He'd got used to having me follow him around and after the summer break I noticed him looking at me in a new way. I'd been flat-chested for so long, but now my body was developing fast and I made the most of my new shape with tight tops and leggings.

THAT BOY

One night the gang went to Hampstead Heath to smoke dope and hang out and Lucien took me for a walk on our own. Once we were out of sight of the others he pushed me against a tree and kissed me. I thought my heart would stop. If death had come then, I would have died in utter bliss.

'Will you go out with me?' he whispered into my hair. I nodded my consent, unable to talk. After that night we became inseparable and I discovered what he was really like. Behind his band persona, he was a very shy but honest person. I started to hang out at his house more than my own. His mother, Anne, was really straightforward and after I introduced her to my mother they became best friends. Anne Hunter, it seemed, had been a bit of a mover and shaker in the Sixties and though it was 1980 she still retained a sparkle, so my mum and her had a lot in common. 'You should do some modelling, Sadie,' Anne said one night when we were all sitting round the dinner table. 'You've got a great look.'

I looked at Lucien, who nodded his approval. A few weeks before, Sarah Dove's father, a fashion designer, had said the same thing. He asked if he could use me, Sarah and Beth as models for his new clothing range for BOY. At the time I'd been too shy to say yes, but now I rang Sarah and said I'd like to do it. The photos came out well, with the three of us looking both punky and doll-like with our heavy make-up and lots of hairspray. Soon I was being used quite regularly for BOY. With the money I got for the photos I paid for a new carpet for my room in Gondar Gardens and started to buy nice clothes. One day, after a shopping trip to the King's Road, a man stopped me at West Hampstead tube station.

'Are you a model?' he said, stubbing out his cigarette.

'Erm, no, why?'

I studied him suspiciously, but he didn't look like a dirty old man and he even had a camera slung over his shoulder.

'I'm a photographer, and you are stunning,' he said, smiling. 'I've got a studio round the corner. If you'd like I could do some professional fashion shots,' he went on, giving me a quick wink.

After mulling it over for a few weeks, I decided to take him up on his offer and Lucien came with me, in case it got tricky. As it turned out, he took some really good shots. 'Take them round some of the model agencies and you'll get work, for sure,' he said after I paid him. He was right: I showed my new portfolio to Askews model agency and to my amazement they took me on. The fact that people wanted to take my photograph was starting to sink in. Soon I started to pick up little photographic jobs. My punk look seemed to go down well, but I realised that I had to look a bit smoother if I wanted to get booked. People were saying that the 1980s were going to be a new style and all of a sudden I had my own money to spend. Soon I'd plunged into a new environment that was exciting all the time. Each day started with phone calls booking me for jobs and the

THAT BOY

bookers telling me I had to go to this address to meet an agency or that studio to be made up and photographed. Having my own money coincided with the beginning of a whole wave of new fashions and I wanted to try everything out and experiment.

At the same time, all my friends were getting into certain drugs, like acid, but it was something I didn't want to do. Some of the older punks were taking heroin, a drug that, as far as I knew, was the worst out there. This group of punks included Lucien's equally beautiful brother Devlin. I had never liked the taste of alcohol and I'd hated the experience with the Tippex and glue sniffing. I never needed to get high but I did it all to fit in with my friends and I certainly never liked any of it enough to do it too much. As for Lucien, he was happy smoking the odd bit of pot. The night I got taken on by the modelling agency I went out to celebrate with Lucien and we met up with Danny Pressman and the gang at a party.

'Wanna get high?' said a guy called Matt, offering me a little tiny square of paper.

'No thanks,' I said, wondering what it was.

A little bit later I began to feel weird. The room started to move and flood with colour. Whatever people had been taking, somehow I'd clearly taken it too. I stared at my drink, trying to pick it up but knocking it over. I staggered outside, looking for Lucien. He was nowhere, not in the party or out in the street. Danny came to look for me and held me up when I tripped. I heard someone say that they wanted to fly, that they wanted to jump out of the window and just go. I thought about that as well.

'Whoa,' I giggled, touching Danny's face. 'You're made of jelly, like a dog.' He smiled and laughed and then helped me back into the party, which for me was made up of rainbows and marshmallow people. Soon the marshmallow melted and I turned to Danny, who seemed to look like the devil. I looked at the clock: it was just after six in the evening.

'I want to go home,' I said suddenly, rushing outside again. Danny and the others must have followed because I was aware of people but I was trapped inside a flicker book of my own life where everything was moving too fast and jerkily. I held my head like it was a piece of precious metal as I ran into McDonald's, which was the worst place I could possibly be, with its fluorescent lights highlighting even whiter faces. In the toilets I looked in the mirror and my face was red and veiny like an alien and my tongue was as dry as sand. All I could do was hold on to the basin.

'Hold on … hold on…' I whispered to myself, feeling tears creep down my cheeks like ants. All the fear, all the terror that I had kept in for 15 years, came out through my skin: the violence, the fights and the things a child shouldn't see. What was in the forefront of my mind was my Dad telling me of his own LSD experience when he'd been spiked. He had suffered psychotic episodes for years afterwards and eventually ended up in a loony bin. I was terrified that the same would happen to me.

THAT BOY

There was a bang on the toilet door. 'Sadie! Are you OK?' Danny and some other lads came in, took me out and got me home, but once I was in my own bed it all got worse. The floor pulled away and again and again I sank into the cellar without moving from my bed.

'Mummy…' I groaned, while Lucien and the others wiped foam from my mouth. It was now three in the morning. I heard Lucien and Danny arguing about what to do.

'We can't tell her mum,' hissed Danny.

'We have to do something, idiot,' said Lucien, clearly angry. 'And who the fuck spiked her with acid anyway?'

'Not me,' replied Danny. 'No way. We need to give her vitamin C – it helps – loads of it.'

Suddenly I had a mouthful of vitamin C tablets, which just made even more foam. They left me to sleep but sleep didn't come, only visions of hell. I was the girl from *The Exorcist* and my father was the devil or an alien and he was trying to kill me. The clock said 8am but as the visions receded it was replaced by a feeling that I was nothing, just a piece of dust, and I had no idea what was real and what was fantasy.

I woke about midday. My room was quiet and after staring at the carpet for a minute I realised that it wasn't going to move. After 18 hours it was over. But it wasn't really over, because over the following days I got frequent flashbacks. Walking down the street I'd suddenly feel like I was back in the hell of that horrific trip. My mind made up awful things and at one point I took a kitchen knife and waited on the sofa for someone to come and get me. Finally I called Dad. We hadn't spoken much since the holiday in France but I was desperate.

'What do I do, Dad?' I pleaded through my tears, and for once he was silent, thinking seriously.

'I think you need to see someone, a therapist. I had to see this fella when I had a bad trip once. I'll give him a ring and you should go along, OK?' Dad said. 'His name is Ronnie Laing.'

The next week I was sitting in an office in Swiss Cottage that belonged to a man who made me nervous straight away, as there was something insincere about his manner. He would smile as I described my fears and pain, instead of showing concern.

He sat opposite me, hands folded on his lap, a calm smile on his face.

'Why don't you tell me what's wrong?' he said after some time. I shrugged and fiddled with my fingers, scared again like a little girl.

'I think I'm paranoid. I'm having hallucinations, like I think someone is going to kill me.'

He frowned and then a weird smile played on his face before he got up and crept round the room, moving cushions and feigning terror and fear.

'Is this what you are doing?' he said. 'Do you fear that someone will jump out every time you move a cushion? Do you look behind doors?'

I shook my head.

THAT BOY

'No? Well then, you aren't paranoid, Sadie. You don't have an anxiety disorder. I think you're just worrying for no reason.'

I went red and remained silent. I felt this man was making fun of me and not taking me seriously. I left feeling humiliated. What good had a visit to a therapist done me? I resolved never to see one again.

Soon afterwards it was my sixteenth birthday and Mum threw a party for me. Holly, my new sister, sat and gurgled in the kitchen and I watched my lovely mum making sandwiches. Holly was the most beautiful baby, with her big green eyes, and I would take her out in her pram, pretending that she was mine. There was a part of me that desperately wanted my own Holly, wanted to settle down with Lucien.

'So, Sadie, I was going to talk to you about your room,' said Mum, looking up from her sandwiches. 'Since you are spending more time with Lucien and also maybe doing more modelling and travelling, maybe we could give your room to the baby?'

My stomach churned and I felt sick. This was the final nail in the coffin: I was being pushed out of my home. I sat in my room staring at the graffitied walls, resisting the urge to go and shout, or even to be bitter and angry at all. It wasn't like I'd grown out of my childhood life, it was more like it had outgrown me and was whispering to me to move on now. It wasn't anything to do with my mother. She was only doing her best, looking after all her kids. I slipped on a tartan mini-skirt and put X-Ray Spex on the tape machine and sang along with Poly Styrene to their song 'Oh Bondage! Up Yours!' In the end I lay on my bed in my claustrophobic teenage bedroom and played air guitar, taking my aggression out on the strings, then breaking the whole guitar into pieces.

'Oiii!' Lucien shouted, knocking on my door before coming in. 'What are you doing hiding in here? The party has started!'

I hitched up my skirt and made it look even shorter and then applied the reddest of red lipsticks. I looked into the dressing-table mirror and gave it a kiss, leaving a residue of lip-shaped paste on the glass. Then I took the lipstick and wrote beside the kiss: 'Sweet Sixteen!'

Soon people started to arrive for the party and someone brought round a chocolate cake with Smarties on top. I cut myself a big slice and started to munch. Before long some of my friends were giggling.

'It's a dope cake,' said one of them. 'It's made with hashish.'

'What?' I said, choking with the shock, as I'd already taken a nibble.

I started to laugh and rolled my eyes. Inside I feared that the acid trip would happen again. Soon I was lying on my bed looking at the pretty cows grazing on my carpet, which was now covered in grass. I couldn't believe that drugs were getting to me again without my wanting them. As soon as the effect of the dope wore off, I made up my mind to move out, not because my mum was making me go but because I felt it was time to take control of my own life and stand on my own two feet. Sweet 16, my arse. It was time to move in across the road with Lucien and his mother.

Soon Lucien and I were acting like we were married. After all my efforts to catch up, I'd left school with a clutch of O-levels. Now I cooked and cleaned for us both and his mum accepted that I was living with them full-time. One afternoon, while cooking for Lucien, I allowed myself a smile and laughed at myself. After everything my mum had been through in her life, it was weird that I had also left home at 16, never to return.

Tenderness

*Tenderness
that I await
of kisses
that make*

*my hairs
awake
to breath
so warm*

*and touch
aloud
of secret
places
of escape*

*to find
this thing
we daren't
begin...*

*Time still
on face
that cuts our
heart.*

CHAPTER FIVE

Finding My Feet

Fade to grey: camera, lights, heat, sweat, the sweet taste of lipstick and hairspray, the feel of mohair and denim, the sound of pop music filling the bleached white studio, Visage, the Specials, Madness, Roxy Music. This was it, this was REAL life...

'Just one more shot, babe,' shouted the photographer, resuming his singalong to the ear-shattering music that filled the studio.

Aching, in pain, struggling to hold the pose, my gums and jaw were in agony from holding the same smile and by determination I managed to make the cramp in my feet go away. Christ ... was this real life?

Finally I heard the shutter snap, that filmy clunk as the image is saved somewhere deep inside the camera.

'Fuckin' brilliant, Sadie, that's it, babe,' said the photographer as he wiped his brow. Every part of my body wilted with relief and I collapsed into the nearest chair and opened my 1981 diary to tick off another assignment. This was one of the many photo sessions that my modelling agency, Askews, had sent me on. I made sure I wrote every single appointment down, as if seeing it there before me in ink made it even more professional. Looking round the studio as the make-up artist and his assistant packed up, I saw my new reality. With this start in modelling I could really be an actress one day. OK, it might only be a little shoot for some teenage magazine, but it was a start. I even made a note of my measurements – hips, boobs, waist and height – and monitored every detail and minute change. This was my new career and I was not going to blow it. I got changed out of the clothes the stylist had put me in and wiped off the make-up. On the downside, the modelling didn't feel as special as I'd thought it would, and the posing, the keeping still, was hard and boring.

In the mirror I examined my unmade-up 17-year-old face: not a line in sight, hair now neatly cut in the latest style, I looked fresh-faced and innocent.

An adult...

In a short time I'd gone from living in a boxroom at my mother's house to being an independent woman who had moved in with her boyfriend. Mum had upped sticks and left London for Ludlow and Dad was in Ashton. Mum was pregnant again and desperate to build a new nest with Bobby in the countryside. Sunshine, Jessie and I stayed behind in London. Sunshine moved in with her boyfriend and Jessie stayed with her dad, Frosty. I'd have rather Mum stayed in London but either I could mope about it or get on with my new life. I felt a rush of pride, then a slight lurch in my stomach. There was no family to fall back on any more, no stability now it was just me, which made my stomach flip. I put a finger on the mirror to trace the shape of my lips, full and red, as every male photographer kept telling me, and smiled.

It all seemed so unreal. Could it really be this easy?

At least now I had my own money, in fact more than I knew what to do with. Even so, I wasn't stupid, and having had nothing for so long, I was determined to hang on to what I now had. I paid a small amount in rent to Lucien's mother and bought some clothes. Actually I bought quite a lot of clothes, but not expensive boutique stuff, more like vintage dresses, shades of the Fifties. I'd been a punk for too long to lose the desire to look different.

The next morning I boarded a train to Ludlow, full of excitement and with presents for Holly. She was now four and a half and growing up so fast. I missed her so much. Mum was pregnant again, which meant that Holly would soon have a brother or sister in a seemingly never-ending cycle of reproduction, but for me, the more children Mum had, the less time I could spend with her. She had a new life now. I sighed and watched the grey of London be replaced by lush green countryside and, at last, by Ludlow. This time, however, I had my own new life and it was too exciting to worry much about what I might be missing out on with my family.

Bobby met me at the station and I chattered non-stop about my recent shoots. When I got to the chocolate-box thatched cottage I saw the attraction of their life there. It was cosy, tiny and very makeshift, with the makings of a vegetable garden. But it was Holly and Mum I was most glad to see and we immediately went outside to look around.

'It's so beautiful here, Mum,' I said taking in a lungful of fresh air.

'I know,' she said, before shivering and heading back indoors where it was warm. We sat down to a home-made cake and a plate of biscuits and I ate guiltily, aware of the calories mounting up and the pressure I put on myself not to gain weight.

'Don't you want to go for a walk or something?' I said, looking at Mum. I'd noticed that she and Bobby spent a lot of time indoors and I couldn't understand it with all the beautiful scenery just outside their door.

'I'm happy in my little house,' she said, humming gently.

'I'll take Holly for a walk,' I said. Already I had a masterplan for my little half-sister: one day she would be a dancer and a gymnast, one day she would have it all and be the best at everything. The next day I went into town and bought her a trampoline for the garden. Mum and Bobby were impressed, and Holly delighted. It was nice to be able to do something for them and now I had the means to do it.

FINDING MY FEET

'Have you spoken to your dad?' said Mum as she kissed me goodbye at Ludlow station a couple of days later. I had to rush back to London for another modelling shoot: a campaign for 7UP.

'No, and I don't really want to either.'

'I know, love,' she said, touching my hair. She knew what had happened in France and how much it had upset me. 'But he keeps calling *me,* asking after you, and I can't keep making excuses for you,' she went on, hugging me goodbye. I ignored her words and got on the train. Once inside I kissed Holly through the glass, both of us with our lips hard to the pane, and watched her saliva trail down the window. Messy. That's how I'd describe my feelings about Dad at that time.

I knew that I couldn't ignore him for ever, because whenever I'd done that in the past he'd just come and found me and muscled in on my friends or turned up at parties and ruined everything. One way to control him was to go and see him first. A few weeks after seeing Mum, I found myself on the train to Manchester, with mixed emotions about seeing his face again. Part of me wanted to stay away, but there was also the part of me that longed for his undivided attention. As soon as he met me off the train all my doubt was forgotten as he picked me up and whizzed me around.

'How's my bloody gorgeous model daughter then, eh? Let me have a lookie at you.' He stood back and took in my clothes. I'd dressed up for the occasion, in a way to show off my new sophistication. I was wearing a vintage leather jacket, jeans and red heels.

There was something not quite right about him, even though he swore he wasn't drinking. I could smell something on his breath, an eerily familiar sickly-sweet smell. His pupils were like pinpricks, almost invisible. Nevertheless we were enjoying the moment and what was the point of ruining the reunion? We drove back to Ashton full of gossip and chatter and when we walked through the door of Dad's house I was flattened by three gorgeous little boys. My angelic trio of long-haired dirty brothers. Anne followed from the kitchen, wiping her hands.

'Sorry about the mess, love,' she said, gesturing at the house. I smiled politely and gave her a hug. The house was a large Victorian place with high ceilings. It stood at the corner of Mossley Road and could have been lovely. Unfortunately it had my dad living in it with all his eccentricities. I could see from Anne's face that she had given up trying to control him. She and Dad went into the kitchen while I played with the boys and I overheard them whispering.

'Have you've been taking it again?'

'Stop nagging me, Anne.'

'I'm not talking about the drink. You know what I mean.'

Then there was silence before a cup of tea arrived. I felt sorry for Anne. She had obviously tried to keep the house tidy but with three unruly boys and Dad, plus Snowy the labrador, it was impossible. Apart from the dirty dishes that the boys had left out, the walls were plastered with photographs and pictures of female genitalia.

'What's all this, Dad?' I said in shock, trying to avert my eyes from the images.

'It's fuckin' art, Sadie. It's beautiful, that's what,' he said, laughing. Anne looked away and I could see she was embarrassed too. I was horrified and felt my cheeks stinging. How could he put me in such an awkward position? I hid my fury and made a start on the washing up and then the floor but no sooner had I mopped it than Toby ran through with five boys from the street. Anne shrugged and picked up a dog-eared novel that was open on the kitchen table. For the rest of the evening she didn't emerge from the book, as if shutting out the chaos. Dad disappeared and left me to fend for myself and the boys.

The next day the weather was beautiful, so I decided to put on my vintage yellow Fifites swimming costume, shades and heels and sunbathed. All I could find to sit on was a broken plastic garden chair. I lay back and put on my shades, flicking through a magazine as Simon, Jamie and Toby ran around me playing football, with Snowy barking. I tried to block out the noise and pretend I was in the South of France. Eventually I gave up and went inside. Dad was slumped on the sofa. He had this way of holding his head in one or both hands, his fingers tensed and splayed like a crab over his face. He would sit like this for hours, as if there was a pain in his head which he was trying to either locate or control. Now he also was drunk and dirty and Anne was wisely avoiding him, sitting in the kitchen reading.

'Sadie, my love, come here and give me a hug,' he said as I tried to tiptoe past him unnoticed.

I looked at him and shrank backwards as he opened his arms to me.

'No,' I said. I was clean and tidy and he was filthy and smelled.

'Why not?' He looked hurt. 'What's up? Don't you love me? I love you more than life. *I made you!*'

I ran upstairs and hid in my room, trying to imagine myself far away. There was something going on with him now that I didn't understand and didn't want to. He seemed to need me too much, to need me to love him and the pressure was all-consuming. Later I crept down with my suitcase and he was still sitting with his head in his hands. I stood at the door and listened as Anne tried to talk to him.

'What's up with you, David? Is it Sadie?'

'She doesn't love me,' he replied sorrowfully, as if he'd given up.

I left a note on the kitchen table and took off. I wanted to put as much distance between me and my dad as I could. I'd had enough of his need, of his crazy art and his drinking. It all repulsed me and I just couldn't deal with it any more.

FINDING MY FEET

Back in London with Lucien I felt like I could breathe again and I immediately called the agency to check for any new bookings.

'Sadie, sweetheart. Guess what. Something big has come up. How do you fancy two months in Japan?' said the booker, with a voice like a machine gun.

As I watched the commuters pouring out of the tube wrapped against the cold I let my mind wander. Japan seemed so exotic and warm. And it was winter in London.

'Me? Japan?'

'Yes, darling, the agency over there loved your look. They can guarantee you lots of campaigns and commercials. You up for it or not?'

Suddenly I thought about Lucien and my heart shut like a vice. How could I survive without the love of my life for two whole months?

'Sadie? You still there? I need to know if you want to go, 'cos we have to act quickly otherwise they'll move on.'

I shut my mind to the images of Lucien and my family and thought about my career. This was the biggest thing that had come up so far and, besides, I was scared of the bookers at the agency, who seemed to have endless 'other girls' they could give my jobs to.

'Yes, er, I'll have to check but, erm, yes, I mean, I'd love to.'

'Great, babe. I'll book you in.'

When I got home I called my mum to ask her permission. Even though I was 17, I still needed parental consent to go abroad with the agency. Mum sounded enthusiastic and her voice really happy, but Holly was crying in the background and a familiar irritation rose inside me, a feeling that I could never have my mother's undivided attention.

'That sounds fantastic, love. Of course you can go. I wish I could come with you,' said Mum.

'You sure?' I said, chewing the inside of my mouth worriedly, thinking about Lucien. 'Two months is ages, Mum, and I'll be all on my own.'

'Of course, darling, but you can always come home if you get lonely. This is a big chance for you.' She paused. 'You've got to go for it.'

I knew that she was as pleased as she sounded and this gave me confidence that I could do it. After all I'd been through with Mum, she was behind me and even if she had other daughters, I comforted myself that I could always confide in her.

'Thanks, Mum,' I said, feeling a rush of closeness to her. This was matched by a rush of guilt as I knew I hadn't made it easy for her to get close to me. It was as if sometimes, in the past I'd withheld affection from her and made it hard to love me. There were times when I'd been selfish and angry for the rows or her boyfriends and I'd played her off against Dad. Now I was on the verge of going to Japan on a huge modelling assignment and being a model left a hollow feeling inside, like I didn't deserve my luck. Everything in Sadie world was always about *me me me*. I pushed the guilt away as quickly as it had come. This wasn't the time for doubt. I had to tell Lucien straight away that I was going. I heard the door slam and rushed to meet him, jumping into his arms and kissing his peroxide-blond hair.

'Guess what!' I said as he twirled me round and round in the kitchen. 'I'm going to Japan!' He stopped immediately and fixed his doe eyes on me, the ice-blue stare cold all of a sudden.

'Without me?' He sounded hurt, accusing, and I pulled him close, nuzzling his neck, this man who was my everything. How could I even think of leaving him for more than 24 hours? But I pulled away and managed to meet his stare.

'It's modelling, it's work. I'll get money for us,' I said, pleading with him not to make this harder for me than it already was.

Later that night we cuddled up and it was as if I was betraying him, and I apologised with every kiss.

'Why don't you come and meet me when the two months are up? We can go travelling?' I said with my head on his chest, listening to his breathing become more regular and rhythmic. While he slept I slid out of bed, pulled on his punk T-shirt and went to make a cup of tea. The kitchen was dark and his mother, Anne, and Devlin were out somewhere. I thought about families, love and loyalty. I studied the photographs of Lucien and Devlin's innocent faces staring back at me. Devlin moved between living in a squat and then coming home when he ran out of money. Anne was very worried about him because he, like the rest of the older punks in the area, was dabbling with harder drugs like heroin. (Anne's concern was, sadly, justified as the beautiful Devlin eventually died of a heroin overdose.) I sat at the kitchen table and looked around the room. No matter how much I loved Lucien's family, I wished that we had our own place where we could live out our fantasy. I fingered the tattoo on my ankle: it was a little bird, and Lucien had one too. We'd got them done together on Finchley Road and caused a near riot when we'd shown them to our parents. No one else had a tattoo at 17, but we'd decided it was a way to seal our love. I opened my diary and let my eyes wander over the pages. It was my bible, and opposite the days and dates I filled the blank pages with photographs and drawings of Lucien, of tickets to bands we'd seen like the Stray Cats, of collages made out of Rizla packets and even notes of various shades of eye shadow. Everything a girl needed from life was in here. Next to the date that the booker had mentioned, I wrote 'JAPAN!' and felt a flutter of nerves.

I knew that however much I would miss Lucien and home, I had to go. Modelling was the bubble of security I needed. If I was to be secure in my new world I had to be financially independent. Lucien seemed happy to just follow along in his old life, with the West Hampstead crew from school. He was a talented musician and with his looks could go far, but he seemed content to hang out and smoke pot. If we were ever going to get our own place, it was going to be me who provided it. But for now, as long as we were together, it was enough. In the absence of my father, I needed constant attention, someone telling me all the time that they loved me, and that was what Lucien did.

Before I left for Japan, a last-minute call came in from the agency to say that the top punk designer Vivienne Westwood wanted me to do her catwalk show. It wasn't something I'd done before and the chance to move and perform instead of just stand and pose for a camera was really exciting. Westwood was famous for introducing staple punk fashion pieces like the Mini-Crini and her signature corset. Backstage at the show with all the other girls, I felt nervous and out of my depth, but it was so frantic and whirlwind there wasn't time to breathe as stylists put me in an outfit and Vivienne herself came by to add finishing touches to the clothes and nod approval. I shot off down the runway, using my well-worn punk attitude and temper and trying to remember all the instructions – mainly, don't be freaked out by all the cameras at the end. When I got to them I stopped and placed a hand on my hip, lifting my chin to the glare of the flash lights, which seemed to go on for an age. But as I turned to go, I realised I wanted to relish the moment just a bit longer and blew a kiss to the applauding audience. Afterwards, as I got changed with the other girls, I felt elated and overheard Vivienne being interviewed for a magazine.

'That's Sadie Frost,' she said. 'She's only 16. All them lips and legs, she's bloody marvellous. She's going to be a star'

Being singled out for praise was confirmation that I had more in me than just being a photographic model.

The next week it was time to go to Japan. Wrenching myself away from Lucien at the airport was horrible but behind my tears I was a wreck of nervous energy. The other models, who were all older than me, were immediately protective of me and I sat watching through the plane window as the tiny speck of England disappeared.

In Japan we had a couple of bookers to chaperone us and were given an apartment to stay in. The shoots proved more challenging than the ones I'd done before because we were on boats offshore, trying to hold poses against the constant motion of the sea. Everything was alien: the culture, the food, even the other girls. Most of them were interested in drinking and partying between shoots. But all I wanted to do was to visit the temples and museums and to explore this fascinating country as I didn't know if I'd be lucky enough to ever see it again.

I called Lucien all the time and told him how much I missed him and my family, but in truth I had plenty to occupy me and worried what it would be like when I saw him again. With this in mind I pushed the travelling idea and bought him a ticket to fly out and join me in Asia. As soon as we had a plan – we would meet in Bangkok and then take the train across Thailand – we felt closer, despite the thousands of miles between us. It seemed so grown-up and sophisticated and leaving Japan to fly to meet him I felt the surge of love rekindled. Unfortunately, the sights and smells of Bangkok didn't match my romantic fantasy. After falling into each other's arms at the airport we booked into a dirty hotel down a smelly sidestreet and realised that even with my money from the shoot we were going to have to rough it while travelling. We had about £500 in traveller's cheques to last us four months.

After four days in the hell-hole of Bangkok we boarded a train to Chang Mai and were met by a guide who was to lead us on a trek into the mountains. We were wide-eyed at everything we saw, the way people lived in the villages and the way that animals just ran free. We stopped for the night in one village and the guide took us to a hut, pointing out a hole in the ground on the way.

'That's the toilet,' he said with a grin, passing me a spliff. I hesitated and looked at it, not wanting to smoke because of my lung and because, well, I never really did, but somehow, out here in the jungle, it seemed OK. I took a toke and inhaled deeply. Ten minutes later I was sparked out on the bed, unable to move or speak.

'I should have warned you, Sadie,' said Lucien, also looking more wide-eyed. 'This skunk shit is way strong.'

'Mmmmmm ugh,' I said, suddenly needing to wee. I went to the shaded hole that the guide had pointed out and prepared to pee, my head feeling as if it was made of lead. I was interrupted by a loud oinking which seemed to be coming from below. I pulled up my pants, moved the straw matting that was covering the toilet and stared at the pig that was happily rolling about in a pile of poo. For a while I thought I might be tripping, and went back to bed.

'You OK, babe?' said Lucien, rolling over to look at me.

'Erm, no. There appears to be a pig in the toilet and it's eating all the poo.'

He burst out laughing at me, until I made him look for himself. It was another part of village life that was wilder than our wildest dreams. After the initial awkwardness of being together after so long apart we fell back into love and into an easy rhythm of knowing what each other was thinking without saying it. We soon ran out of money but just as we did we arrived at a paradise beach where we shared a small hut with some other travellers, living on bananas and tins of Carnation milk. I was completely free and my life was mine. Lucien completed me and I believed that I could take on his outlook: that we had to just 'let life happen' and not try to achieve.

The trouble was, that just wasn't me. I tried, but when we got back to England new modelling assignments started to pile up and I was featured in shoots for *ID*, *The Face*, *Marie-Claire* and *Vanity Fair*. With me extra busy and Lucien doing the same old thing, I knew we were drifting apart again. I was too eager to get wherever life was taking me to be laid-back like Lucien, and besides, I'd seen my parents live like that and they hadn't achieved their dreams. My new dream was to get a place of my own.

FINDING MY FEET

It was the beginning of 1983 and there was an air of promise in London. People kept talking about the recession being over and, although I wasn't sure what that meant for me, it was clear that punk music was dying out and being replaced by New Romantic bands like Wham!, Spandau Ballet and Duran Duran. One day, I also got a call from the agency that had me jumping with excitement.

'The director of this pop video wants to see you for a casting, babe,' said the booker. 'He's called Duffy and it's for the new Spandau video.'

I could hardly contain myself: not only were Spandau Ballet the band of the moment but it meant doing some acting, and surely this would lead down the right path for me. I arrived at the audition more nervous than I'd been since Italia Conti but I tried not to show it. Duffy was in a room with Gary Kemp, Spandau's guitarist, and the photographer looked me over as I approached their chairs.

'Right, Sadie, listen, babe, we want you to listen to this music and just move,' he said, fiddling about with the tape player.

'Move?' I said, confused.

'Yeah, y'know, express yourself. Pretend you are a sunflower and sort of grow.'

As the music of 'Gold' came on, I tried to take on board what Duffy had said, dancing with abandon round the room, being a sunflower. I felt stupid and embarrassed, thinking it was a childish thing to do, but when it was all over Gary smiled and winked at me, causing me to blush all over. Later that night the agency called. 'Sadie, Duffy loved you. They want you in the video, so pack your bags, girl, you're going to Spain.'

So my sunflower act had worked and I jumped about my bedroom, repeating the trick, realising that perhaps I was a pretty good actress after all. Even if I'd felt stupid during the rehearsal I'd taken it on the chin and put myself out there and I was proud. The next week I met the video crew and we flew out to Seville. We were filming in the desert, where many Spaghetti Westerns had been shot. No sooner had we arrived than I felt like I was drowning. I felt out of place among the crew and the band, who seemed to speak a different language. Nothing was familiar and I was a fish out of water. At home I was in control; out here I had no reference points and floundered. Still, I did my best to perform in the video, which involved me being sprayed in gold paint and leaping unseen along balconies like a spy. The video was a spoof on the James Bond film *Goldfinger*: I was the Bond girl and Tony Hadley the Bond character. I lay there as the make-up artist applied the last touches of gold paint, with the sweltering lights pointed towards me. The sound recordist pressed playback and Tony's guttural voice sang, 'The man with the suit and the case, you're indestructible.' Throughout the shoot Gary was really kind and attentive to me, but I still felt like the little kid in a room full of adults. Most of the time I wore my mini-skirt and attracted constant glances from the crew as I went to get my lunch from the service table.

'Ignore them,' said Gary, as I blushed heavily and sat down to eat. 'Why don't you come out for a walk with me, when we get back to London?'

'I can't,' I said, my face colouring up out of control. 'I've got a boyfriend.'

Gary nodded and smiled and went back to his lunch, taking the news in his confident stride.

When I got home I was glad to be back on my patch, with Lucien's arms around me again. And most importantly, I now had enough money to put down a deposit on my own flat. I soon found a place I liked in West Hampstead and put in an offer. I was so excited that I drew a picture of the floor plan in my diary so I could carry it round with me and plan the decor. Once I'd bought the flat I spent the next few months painstakingly doing it up. It was as if all my childhood dreams of having my own boudoir were coming true. I used old vintage bits and bobs to make it utterly feminine, contrasting this look with dark, heavy curtains. Of course I knew that I needed a flatmate to help with the mortgage payments, so I rang an old school friend called Abby Hoffman and she agreed to move in straight away. We'd always got on well and I thought she would make a good housemate as we were interested in the same things, like dance and fitness.

My focus was totally on my career, and mainly on dancing. I attended classes at Pineapple in Covent Garden and the Urdang Academy, and me and Abby would spend the entire time hanging out in our dance tights drinking tea and, we thought, living the high life. Lucien still gravitated towards his West Hampstead friends and we found it harder to be together, but I wasn't about to give up on our love. We started hanging out in Dalston with some of the young trendy fashionistas and musicians. One particular party was banging, the music was loud, and I was struck by a beautiful blonde girl who kept looking at me, then looking away. I did the same to her, all the time draping myself over Lucien and needing his full attention.

'Who's that girl?' I asked him, intrigued by the blonde because I related to her in a way I couldn't explain. Sometimes you just see people from a distance and know they mean something to you, even before you've spoken to them. This girl was very well groomed and confident, with sleek looks like a cat. Lucien shrugged, but I didn't give up and found a reason to go over and talk to her.

'I'm Sadie,' I said, trying not to sound stupidly nervous. 'Who are you?'

'Jemima French,' she said, half-smiling, checking me out.

Lucien stood in the other corner, moodily watching my newfound readiness to socialise. I wanted him, but I felt restricted, only allowed to do the same old things he still wanted to do. There were new people to meet and adventures to have. Like with Jemima. On the way home Lucien refused to talk.

'What is it?' I asked, fearing the answer, but again he shrugged.

'Dunno, I just feel like I'm not enough for you any more.'

I threw my arms round this beautiful boy and covered him in kisses like confetti, but underneath I was scared: scared of losing him, but also scared of not moving on.

As a way of befriending Jemima, I asked her if she'd do a modelling shoot with me the next week. It went well and before I knew it, she'd cut her long, blonde hair short and dyed it black like mine. It was like we were the positive and negative of each other, experimenting with clothes and different looks. Soon Abby moved out of my flat. We'd become far too competitive. I didn't like the fact that she was better at dancing than I was, and then everything became a rivalry: what we ate, drank, dieting, everything. Besides, I wanted to spread my wings and party. Inside the devil that was my father started to dance to his own tune and I wanted to dance along with it. One girl with a similar urge to party was Tracy Buckley, another model. She moved into my flat almost immediately we met and she introduced me to Crazy Larry's, a club on the King's Road that was suddenly the place to be, along with the Café de Paris and the Wag. Suddenly I was being invited to dinners and put on the guest list of various clubs. My face, which had appeared in Spandau's 'Gold' video, was seemingly the face that fitted the moment. By then I'd done a lot of advertising campaigns and my face was on billboards across London for 7UP and other things. In no time I'd turned again from a homely girl living with her boyfriend to a wild party girl with no ties and no desire for any.

There was only one problem – Lucien. One night I crept into my bed after a night out with Tracy at Crazy Larry's and found Lucien up and smoking a spliff. I didn't say a word, just made us some tea, and we sat staring at the floor. There was barely an inch of space between us but the emptiness echoed like an abyss.

'So, I reckon that's it, then, yeah? I mean, don't you love me no more?' he said mournfully.

'Of course I love you … it's just…' I didn't need to finish the sentence. We both knew we'd been pretending already for months; there wasn't anything left. In a way he'd had the best of me and the worst. I had a feeling that I'd been a nightmare to live with – selfish and needy; but he'd also been my saviour, my security against the past. In the end, that past, my dad, was too deep inside me for him to save me from it. He just wasn't strong enough to compete with my dad.

As a way of dealing with the split I threw myself into my modelling. I would go to the West End every day, do a shoot if one was booked, then pop into my new modelling agency, Select Models, and see if there was any new work. It was there I met Zoe Grace, another punky-looking girl who, like me, had a Mohican hairdo, and like me, wasn't stick-thin. I was intrigued by her black hair and black eyes and the far-out things she'd say. One day she announced that she was going to marry David Bowie. She said it with such conviction I didn't doubt her for a minute. We both got called 'Thunder Thighs' by the bookers, who constantly told us to lose weight. Not that we needed to.

Zoe had a flat round the corner from the agency, in Great Titchfield Street behind Oxford Street, and there she would put on some punk music and read my tarot cards. The place would smell of incense and crazy herbal mixes.

'You're gonna meet a new man that drives you crazy,' she said as she turned over a card one day.

'Am I really? Who? What's his name?' I pressed her, unable to imagine falling in love again after Lucien.

'Fuck knows,' said Zoe, grinning, 'but we better get down to Crazy Larry's tonight just in case he's there.'

The door bell rang. It was Tracy Buckley, come to hang out, and the three of us tried on clothes and got excited about the night ahead. It was Friday and that meant the beginning of a long alcoholic weekend of partying. The phone rang and interrupted our preparations.

'Oh, hey, Robert,' said Zoe lazily, putting her hand over the phone and mouthing 'Robert Perino' at us. Tracy and I smiled at each other. Robert was the king of the nightclub scene, running the coolest club nights at venues all over London. He specialised in knowing young good-looking girls, and if you got a call from Robert it meant you got your cab paid to the club and didn't buy a drink all night.

Later we turned up at Crazy Larry's dressed up to the nines in a cab paid for by Robert. We stepped out on to the kerb like royalty as the bouncers parted a waiting group of punters to let us in. Across the road, three lads stood together smoking. One of them was wearing a cool hat and caught my eye. He smiled and my heart did a little lurch. Later on the three boys showed up in the club. They were all good-looking and cool in a different way to the Hampstead skater boys: they seemed more sophisticated, with long hair and dagger-like stares. Eventually the one in the hat came over and we made room for him to sit with us in the little booth.

'I'm Gavin,' he said, grabbing my hand and kissing it. It turned out that Gavin Rossdale and his mates, Sacha Puttnam and Mark Armstrong, were Westminster School boys who were in a band called Midnight. They invited us out with them the next night to Pucchi Pizza on the King's Road and instantly we all got on. They offered us a new kind of fun as they had cars and knew things and people that I hadn't met before – rich and powerful people who had big houses in the country.

'Fancy a weekend away?' said Gavin the next week. I knew that Zoe's prediction was true: I'd meet a man and fall in love.

'A weekend where?'

'Thought we could all drive out to the country and stay at my friend's place.'

'Cool.' I tried to sound relaxed but inside I was bursting with excitement.

On the Friday night me, Zoe and Jemima piled into Gavin's car with Sacha and Mark and headed out of London, drinking wine from the bottle while the cassette player belted out the Eurythmics song 'Sweet Dreams'. That weekend we swam in the outdoor pool and played games, lazed around and talked. I was more and more taken by Gavin, who clearly knew the effect he had on women. Zoe sidled up to me. 'Gavin fancies you,' she whispered.

I shot her a mad look.

'No he doesn't.'

'Yes he does. You have this weird effect on men.'

'No I don't,' I snapped back, not wanting to think I had any 'effect' on men.

'Yes you do, so get used to it,' she said, grabbing a can of lager and heading out to the pool.

I'd never really thought about this and her words caused me to think. Me and Gavin? I shook my head. Gavin already had a girlfriend, a gorgeous editorial model called Lindsey Thurloe who was an English Beatrice Dahl lookalike. He was off-limits but we became close friends anyway, interested in each other but never able to do anything about it. Besides, he was dangerous, casually seeing many girls and seeming to have them all on a string. On the other hand, his most regular girlfriend, Lindsey, was the girl I wanted to become. She was wild, dynamic, intelligent and crazy, a sort of Betty Blue. She was difficult and didn't care what people thought about her. Hanging out with her made me realise – I wanted to be difficult too. Inside me the ghost of David Vaughan stirred...

I was nearly 21 and Lucien was now a distant memory. Spandau Ballet even invited me to appear in their new video for the song 'Fight For Ourselves' and I agreed instantly. Since the 'Gold' video I'd always been a bit in awe of Gary and the others and saw it as a way of keeping my film aspirations alive. I also took my partying to a new level, not that I really enjoyed drinking and I always kept away from drugs, but I suddenly got a taste for champagne and the high life. I decided to hold my twenty-first birthday party at Crazy Larry's. It was 1986 and the new bands on the block were INXS and Curiosity Killed The Cat. It seemed a good idea to share my party with another model, Caroline Dodd, as that way we would be able to fall back on each other if no one turned up! We needn't have worried: the place was rammed when we arrived in dresses designed to kill. Mine was made of purple crushed velvet and fitted my body like a glove. Mum had come down from Ludlow specially for the party and had left behind Holly and the new addition to our family, Jade Rose Hope. I took her to pick out my birthday present in South Molton Street, *the* place to shop in London. She was excited about my party and seeing me again. Like Holly, Jade was a stunning baby, only a few months old at the time, and I mooned over the photos, desperate to see her again. Meanwhile Mum and I chattered and stared at all the jewellery in Butler & Wilson. Mum was impressed by my new sophisticated tastes and knowledge. I picked out a gold and silver matching necklace and she bought it for me. It was my first proper piece of jewellery ever.

'I'm so proud of you, my gorgeous daughter,' she said with a smile, the old sparkle back in her pretty eyes, and we hugged. It seemed that some of the harm from the past was healing. Certainly I knew I hadn't made it easy for her, and she'd been so young a mum that she'd hurt me without meaning to. That evening at my party the champagne flowed and Jemima, Zoe and Tracy danced on the tables. I got up on a table alone and started to dance seductively to the audience below.

'Sexy Sadie!' shouted Miggy, the drummer from Curiosity Killed The Cat. Miggy had been following me round all night and asking me for a date. Since he was in such a cool band, I was very flattered. I enjoyed the attention of the crowd watching me as I danced. This was the kind of attention that I craved and hey, I was 21! What else mattered?

Over the next few months my partying with the model set began to wear a little thin. There was a new legal drug around, MDMA, that had come over from New York, and everyone was experimenting with it. Someone offered me some at the Café de Paris and I was told it was a legal drug from America, used to encourage feelings of love between couples. I was aware that it felt nice, as if the sun was warming your body, but even though I tried it then and a few more times, I was never really interested in it. All of a sudden the party crowd looked like they were being taken over by drugs and drink. But it just wasn't *me*. I'd seen too much as a kid to want the chaos that I knew could start with drugs. The effect of MDMA might have been pleasant but it would wear off quickly, leaving a low that reminded me of a black place inside me – a whole boxful of paranoia that I'd closed off after my ill-fated visit to the therapist when I was 16. A couple of weeks after my first MDMA experience, the government made it illegal but that didn't stop it spreading though the club scene.

One night at the Café de Paris I looked around me, at the models and the bright young things all off their heads, and wondered what I was doing, where I was going. All of a sudden tears overwhelmed me and I found a dark corner and sat and wept. Who was I now? My whole work ethic was getting lost, the pureness of working on my dance, and the security and loyalty of Lucien and my West Hampstead friends were gone.

'Sadie? Sadie?' I was aware of my name being called and looked up from the flood of tears.

'Are you OK?' said the voice. I wiped my eyes and saw that it belonged to Gary Kemp. He smiled kindly and knelt down to talk to me.

'Yeah, I'm fine,' I lied. 'Just some dickhead bloke messing me around, that's all.'

'You don't need that,' he said, handing me a tissue.

'No,' I said, blowing my nose. 'No I don't.'

We looked at each other for a moment, and something

passed between us. He took me outside and found me a taxi, and before it drove off he asked for my number. As I gave it to him I had a weird feeling in my stomach. For the first time in ages I felt safe.

CHAPTER SIX

Love and Marriage

Nineteen eighty-seven. Gary's mysterious appearance that night at the Café de Paris was in some ways a miracle. He was like a giant sticking plaster which I immediately applied to all my problems. It was as if, with Gary there, something in my head got fixed. Covered over were the insecurities about being a paranoid wreck, gone were the negative thoughts about my body and my damaged mind. Actually not gone, just hidden, not from the world but from myself.

After my appearance in the Spandau videos I'd lost contact with Gary, despite there being a flicker of interest on both our parts. A few months before seeing Gary at the Café de Paris, I was sitting having a cup of tea with Jemima at her new house in Grove Terrace, Highgate, when she mentioned that she'd bumped into him while she was out jogging.

'He lives just a few doors down. Exciting, huh?' she said, giggling. My ears immediately pricked up.

'Let's go jogging and see if we can bump into him again,' I said, feeling a prickle of adrenalin. Jemima agreed at once and I had a hunch that she too had a soft spot for him. We planned to run the coming weekend and I turned up in full make-up and designer running gear.

'You look like you're going to a bloody fashion shoot, not a gentle jog over the Heath,' said Jemima, checking me out. 'I don't know why you're bothering. We probably won't even see him,' she added, doing up her laces, and I shot her a wry smile.

A few minutes later as we jogged past Gary's house we slowed right down and amazingly there he was, just coming out of his front door. We stopped and faked breathlessness, pretending that we'd been running for ages. Gary looked amused to see the two of us out jogging and as we talked I sensed a mutual curiosity as we caught each other's eye, but we didn't exchange numbers and parted with a casual goodbye.

It wasn't until our encounter at the Café de Paris that everything fitted into place. Gary was pretty but he was also so wise and manly, polished and clean. His pristine eyes twinkled and gleamed with a sureness of who he was and he didn't intimidate me in the same way as the other men I'd been dating. A few days after we met at the club, he called and we talked. I didn't want to rush into anything and nor did he. He'd been in another relationship and it was coming to an end. Our first date quickly led to the second, a few nights later, and the third to the fourth. He

LOVE AND MARRIAGE

took me back to his place, a big Georgian house in Grove Terrace, and showed me around. I couldn't quite believe that this sophisticated man was interested in me. His house was a mirror of his mind: it was grand and Classical in décor, but also influenced by William Morris and full of heavy, dark furniture in the Arts and Crafts style. Rossetti paintings hung on the walls and it was like a museum or the house of a private collector. I slowly began to see myself there, with him. Our hands touched as I slid mine down the stair rail. He looked at me and smiled.

'You like it?' he said, and as he did I felt the edge of his breath tickle my cheek, fresh and sexy.

'Yeah, I love it.'

He leaned forward and kissed me on the lips. There was no point in resisting and I allowed myself to be completely swallowed up in his dream. The next two weeks were like a cotton-wool paradise as Gary showered me with love. Always attentive, he constantly gave me compliments, and most of all, I was sure of his affection and felt secure. At the end of the second week he told me that his relationship was definitely over as we gazed at each other over dinner at Le Caprice, a chic restaurant in Piccadilly that was full of glamorous ladies and had modern art on the walls. Gary had bought me an Azzedine Alaïa dress for the occasion and I tried not to feel too uncomfortable next to all the beauty I saw. I was still awkward of my post-teenage looks and my mouth was way too big for my face, but Gary didn't care. He grabbed my hand and smiled.

'Move in with me,' he whispered, leaning forward into the light.

'What?' I said, knocked back with surprise and delight.

'Well, why wait? We're in love, aren't we?' His eyes twinkled, my vision blurred. I think I nodded before he kissed me again, not being able to believe my good luck to have been swept off my feet by a cockney Prince Charming and to be moving in with him just three weeks after being such a pathetic mess at the Café de Paris. I went home and got a few things together before Gary helped me organise the move properly and rent out my place.

On the night of 15–16 October 1987 we awoke to the sounds of a terrible storm and in the morning went to the Heath to survey the damage. Many trees had been torn away from the ground like matchsticks, and Gary returned home and wrote a song about the storm, which he dedicated to me. That storm and the song were a moment that seemed to sum up and seal our relationship and make it stronger.

Straight away after moving into Grove Terrace I got on with making the house more homely and giving it a woman's touch with my own style – the boudoir theme, dark and luxurious, with perfume and lace, that had started way back when I was a seven-year-old swiping antique perfume bottles from my mother's market stall. This was a welcome distraction from my modelling career, which was coming to an end. I'd had enough of it and felt that my future lay in acting and luckily, about the same time, the offers of shoots dried up and I didn't push it with the agency. I auditioned for a part in a new play in Manchester and to my complete surprise I got it. I'd never expected to as my insecurity made me measure myself as coming up short next to more trained and polished actresses. I'd left Italia Conti early and even while I was there I'd felt that I was somehow less than others, not as confident and vivacious as my peers such as Frances Ruffelle and Amanda Mealing.

This part was my big chance and I accepted it with delight. It also meant going to live in Manchester for a few months and this brought mixed emotions. As I travelled up on the train, a journey now so familiar to me, I knew that Dad wanted me to live with him for the run of the play, but I saw this as a chance to assert my independence. I was dating a clever, brilliant man and considered myself elevated in some way by my new lifestyle, but at the same time I was looking forward to spending some time with Dad, even if I didn't want to stay with him.

The play, *Mumbo Jumbo*, was to be directed by Nicholas Hytner and the leading man was a young actor called Michael Grandage. Dad and Anne met me at the station and I lost no time in filling them in on the play, my plans and Gary. As they drove me to Mossley Road there was silence after I announced that I wasn't going to stay there but wanted to rent my own place. But later Dad helped me find a bedsit in the city centre and dropped me off there before rehearsals started. 'Bye then, love,' he said, leaning to kiss me, but I just scooped up my case and ran into my new digs. 'Can I come and see the play?' he shouted after me. 'If you want,' I said, trying to get the key in the door. Once inside I knew I was being quite cold but I didn't care: it was as if it was time for him to be hurt as payback for all the times he'd hurt me.

On the first night of the play, as we waited in the wings for our first scene, there was great excitement. My costume was school uniform and pigtails and the clothes and make-up made me feel innocent again. The nervous feeling was so intense that I stepped away from my body, not knowing how I was going to propel myself on to the stage in front of the lights. In the end the stage manager gave me a little push, otherwise I'd have missed my entrance. Then something took over, a higher power that made sure I got the first line out and everything flowed after that. The part I wasn't looking forward to was kissing Michael Grandage full on the lips, but I convinced myself it was only acting and Gary wouldn't mind. When it came to the final curtain I took my bow elated, searching the audience for familiar faces. Dad and Anne waved, but something just made me turn and walk away, not even acknowledging my dad. This behaviour was becoming firmly established between us: I would reject him, then some time later I would accept him again. It was like an iron curtain had come down in my head, separating me from my love for him. It both hurt and pleased me to see his forlorn face as I rejected him.

Gary came up to see the play and was always very

supportive of my career. Soon after, I was cast for a part in the film *Diamond Skulls*, starring Gabriel Byrne and Amanda Donohoe, a thriller based loosely on the Lord Lucan story. I played Rebecca, a spoilt, fun-loving upper-class beauty. It was quite a role to get my teeth into. After the filming I was expecting more offers but none came. Not that I minded, because in my head the need to change was there and a change was taking place once more. It was as if I had to reject everything I had become and settle down and be mumsy, as if I was fulfilling the part of me that was in my mother. I was in love with a man who was in love with me. His generosity seemed to know no bounds. One afternoon he led me outside the house and put his hands over my eyes, and when I opened them I was looking at a blue VW Beetle impossibly tied up in a yellow bow. What the neighbours thought of this extravagance was beyond me. I threw my arms round Gary and kissed the life out of him. There was no end to these romantic gestures, and one weekend he whisked me to the Cliveden Hotel, telling me to pack the new dress and lacy underwear that he'd come home with. One grey day I got a message to pack a bag and meet him at Waterloo station. I turned up to see, amid the hustle and bustle of commuters, Gary standing at the entrance to the special platform that housed the Orient Express.

'But I haven't got any clothes,' I said as he grabbed my hand and my bag.

'What did you bring in here then?' he asked, confused. I

shrugged. I'd thrown in a pair of knickers and one dress, not enough for a grand tour to Venice.

'It doesn't matter, we'll get you more,' he said, smiling and squeezing my hand.

My life had become like the Orient Express, a luxurious bubble that rolled smoothly along a track. It was as if I was watching life go by out the window of my own train; its grey drudgery was only fleeting, so cushioned was I behind my protective 'Gary glass'. A few weeks later Gary proposed. At that moment my train came to a halt. Up until then I'd been swept along but now suddenly real life came rushing in. Who was I? What did this mean?

'Sadie?' said Gary, staring into my eyes, willing me to answer the most important question. 'Will you?'

'Um er, um well...' I mumbled, ill at ease, unconnected to the present. All I could think about was the past. My family's relationships flashed in front of my eyes: I had never known happy marriages. Then I leapt from the past to worrying about the future and I could only think about what could go wrong. All my life I'd made an effort not to live in the real world because I never trusted reality to serve up happiness. It was also because of the brainwashing my father had given me about it being 'me against the world', a world that would 'only enslave people'. Up to that moment the Gary fairy tale had allowed me to continue to avoid reality. But marriage? That was reality *and* responsibility.

'Sadie?' he asked again, looking for an answer.

'Oh, I dunno. Yeah, maybe.'

LOVE AND MARRIAGE

It wasn't that I didn't love Gary. I did, I just didn't truly understand the concept of love because of my past. I put off the decision and when he asked me again a few days later, I accepted properly. Gary understood why I'd stumbled over my words and knew that it was a big decision for me, and, after all, I was younger than him. When we told the other members of Spandau Ballet and their wives, there was a cry of shock from some of them. Some of the wives cried, as they cared a lot for Gary and saw me as this young foolish girl, fond of her Kir Royales and a bit mouthy. It was all so sudden, not two months after we'd first dated and of course they thought we were rushing into it. Luckily for me, Shirlie of the girl band Pepsi and Shirlie, the wife of Gary's brother Martin Kemp, decided to take me under her wing. I was grateful for that because it was hard being catapulted into the world of a famous band and suddenly having dinner at L'Escargot with people like Bob Geldof and George Michael.

The wedding was to be arranged according to my wishes, and what I wanted was a modest country wedding in the village of Stanton Lacy, near my mother's house. Mum had now established a wonderful family life in Shropshire and, after all the years of hurt and unhappiness, she seemed to have found security with Bobby, Holly and Jade. She'd even moved her parents, Tom and Betty, up the road to retire. The only cloud on the horizon as I prepared for my big day was Dad. I chose not to invite him to the wedding; our relationship was still intensely volatile – he was still drinking and I couldn't trust him not to upset someone. So I asked Grandpa Tom to give me away. All my sisters were the perfect bridesmaids, dressed in pink satin. They were all very well behaved apart from Jade, who refused the wedding dinner and ordered a boiled egg and soldiers.

Gary came from a big working-class Irish family from north London, and for him closeness to the family was very important. In his mother's house the women did the cleaning and looked after their men. I loved spending time with his parents, Frank and Eileen, who took me in as their own. But sometimes I would catch Eileen looking at me strangely, so I asked her what was wrong.

'Oh nothink, darling!' she'd say, narrowing her eyes. 'It's just you remind me of that Liza Minnelli.' I took this to mean that she thought I was a bit precious, a bit of a performer – or at least rather strange. Gary extended his strong sense of family to my own, treating them all with affection.

Despite Gary's wealth, I was still very easy to please. I enjoyed being spoiled for the first time in my life but I was always suspicious of spending too much. I went to the King's Road with Zoe and Jemima and bought a conservative wedding dress by David Fielding which was a cute Fifties cut, very fresh and clean-lined in the Audrey Hepburn style. We hired the village hall for the reception and Gary organised a fireworks display. It was the perfect day and

LOVE AND MARRIAGE

afterwards we slipped, like a hand into a glove, into a perfect married life.

We got an old English sheepdog called Lola that I carried around in a basket. Lola and I had matching ribbons and scarves and took to charming the local shopkeepers together. Soon I'd converted Gary to vegetarianism and yoga. He let his hair grow long and we slowly morphed into each other, becoming slightly hippy in our ways. I quickly abandoned all my old friends and clubbing life to settle into 'being a couple'. Gary could be very controlling and headstrong but I didn't complain because we were in love. In no time it was as if I was middle-aged, getting up at the same time every day and going to the gym with Gary, wearing cardigans and going to pottery classes. Sometimes he'd tell me what to wear and what to do.

Not that our life lost its romance: Gary wrote songs for me and plied me with poems and I felt like I was in an old-fashioned romantic novel. He loved to walk and we often went to the Lake District and donned anoraks and climbed mountains. I was completely happy, yet there was a small part of me that wanted to rebel against this and wear pink stockings and hang out in clubs. I convinced myself, however, that this was just the destructive part of me that I had to suppress. I was behaving like a mature, responsible adult but I also felt crushed by the weight of it and, even though Gary was my anchor, I began to feel a bit smothered.

Around that time Gary landed the role of Ronnie Kray,

alongside his brother Martin as Reggie Kray, in a film about the East End criminal twins. The producers of *The Krays*, Dominic Anciano and Ray Burdis, took us to the Groucho Club in Soho, a new media den where we would hang out and drink. They offered me a role in the film as well and I was honoured, because even though the part was small it meant acting alongside Steven Berkoff. It was an exciting time as Gary and Martin embraced their roles and I watched my husband transform into a gangster, albeit temporarily. The premiere of the film, in Leicester Square, was a star-studded occasion. I chose an Azzedine Alaïa dress, got my hair curled and had my make-up done by a make-up artist. On our arrival in Leicester Square the photographers shouted and for a second I felt like a movie star. I loved Gary's success and he was so great at making me feel special.

From time to time Dad would turn up at our front door in Grove Terrace and announce he was staying. For the first time I had a father figure of my own who could protect me, and Gary would – in the nicest possible way – frighten my father into either going away or behaving. Even so, Gary was too nice to deny him a bed, even though his shoes would go missing when Dad left. I'd call Dad and ask him if he'd seen them and he'd laugh and say, 'Yeah, I'm bloody borrowin' 'em for a bit.'

Finally there came an evening when Dad overstepped the mark. It was on his home territory, when Spandau were doing a gig at the Manchester Apollo. Even after all the

LOVE AND MARRIAGE

times he'd 'borrowed' Gary's clothes and shoes, Gary had a lot of respect for Vaughany as an artist and invited him along to the gig. Halfway through the set Dad wandered on to the stage drunk out of his skull and had to be dragged off by security men. I wanted the ground to open up because he looked like an old drunken tramp and he'd managed to destroy all Gary's trust and respect. Despite that evening, we still had my half-brothers Simon, Jamie and Toby to stay whenever they came to London to see me. Simon even stayed with us while he was studying architecture in London.

It was on New Year's Eve 1990, while we were having a romantic walking holiday in the icy Lake District, that I conceived Fin. We snuggled by the fire and blew frosted breath at each other and were completely happy. Four weeks later, when I realised that I was one hundred per cent pregnant, I told Gary, who was elated. It was the news we both needed. It seemed to seal our relationship and allowed me to put my nervousness to one side and throw myself into something new – being a mother. During the nine months nothing went wrong and I bloomed into my new, rounded skin. Of course Gary insisted on the best care and I was booked into a private hospital in Hendon under the care of Yehudi Gordon, who was one of the best obstetricians in the business. One Friday in my ninth month – on my actual due date – I began to have contractions. We'd planned everything and had a bag packed and all my outfits chosen. Weirdly, I wasn't at all scared, because of my lifelong enjoyment of being in hospital and also because I knew I had a high pain threshold. Part of me even liked it. On the North Circular the contractions started getting closer together.

'Get a move on,' I urged Gary, who was getting whiter by the minute. When we pulled into the hospital we were rushed in to see the midwife, who took one look at me and said, 'Go home, you're not in labour.'

I had a feeling in the base of my spine as if someone had put a lead weight on my lower back which forced me to walk on tiptoe. I knew something was happening.

'Er, can you just check me over, please?' I implored the midwife, knowing I didn't want to get back into the Range Rover. She agreed and once she'd got me on the treatment table she was forced to eat her words.

'Oh, gosh! You're five centimetres dilated,' she said. 'That's unbelievable.'

I was pleased that it was finally happening and I got into the birthing pool.

'Come on, Gary,' I said, between contractions, and held out my hand to him. He looked like a free spirit with his long hair and beard, the new look he was cultivating at the time.

'Coming, babe,' he said, jumping into the pool with me and holding my hand. The nurses must have been amused to see us in the water like a pair of hippies rather than a yuppie couple, but we were too busy to care, and seven hours later Finlay arrived. As they wrapped him and put

LOVE AND MARRIAGE

him on my chest, I stared in wonder at this little white baby. He had the porcelain skin of Gary's Irish heritage and was the most incredible, wonderful thing I'd ever held. Nothing had prepared me for the way I'd feel that first night in the hospital with Finlay in the cot beside me, my pale little Irish bruiser. We named him Finlay Munro, after the hill we'd climbed in the Lake District, where he was conceived. I took to breastfeeding and motherhood like a duck to water. It satisfied the yearning I'd felt when I looked after my baby sisters Jessie, Holly and Jade as my own.

As soon as I got Fin home all my girlfriends and my mother rallied round, providing tea, gossip and hotpot. But after they had all left, I was on my own again and the house seemed very big and empty. I would sit on the sofa and feel like it had a plughole and that I was being sucked down into it. No one could tell me why I felt so low. I would sit there breastfeeding and feel as if I was being drawn into the very fabric, held in place, unable to move, by the force of my feelings. I felt useless: a wife and mother but not up to the job. I didn't know who I was any more. I'd lost the part of my personality that made me *me*, the independent career woman. Where had she gone?

When Fin was seven or eight months old I had a call out of the blue. It was from my old agent, who had been contacted by some producer in Los Angeles.

'Hey, Sadie, you need to get to LA as soon as possible.'

'But I can't. I mean, I've got my baby and, well, what's it for anyway?'

'It's a screen test for a movie.'

'What movie?' I said, only half listening as I was trying to feed Fin. It was so long since I'd had any sniff of acting work that I didn't really buy anything he was saying.

'*What movie?* It's bloody Francis Ford Coppola, baby, and he wants to meet you!'

I stood in the kitchen and spooned food into my baby son, trying to keep my feet on the ground. Apparently *Diamond Skulls* had just come out in the States and was getting good reviews but, more importantly, I was getting good reviews. Coppola had seen it and looked me up. I told Gary when he got home and he hugged me and urged me to go.

'You've got to go, babe. It's a great opportunity and I'll even pay for your flight,' he said, but right now Fin had my attention and I picked him up and held him tight. This was everything I wanted but could I leave my baby and fly into the unknown?

The answer had to be yes. I needed a new challenge and this answered my inner longing to rediscover my identity. Gary assured me that he and Fin would follow me out there should I get the role, and besides, it was only a screen test and I would probably be home before I knew it.

On the plane to the States I studied the script and the character profile for the part I was up for in the blockbuster *Bram Stoker's Dracula*. Lucy Westenra was an exhibitionist

LOVE AND MARRIAGE

with no inhibitions and a wild side. All of a sudden I regretted my new life, because, had I been auditioning for this role before I'd met Gary, I'd have fitted that description to a T. Now I was a mother with a body that was still plump and saggy from childbirth, and even if it wasn't true, that was how I felt.

'Hi, I'm Lucy Westenra.' I looked in the vast mirror at the Beverly Hills Hotel and tried to be convinced by the person staring back at me. I readjusted the socks inside my bra and took another look. I pouted, decided it wasn't perfect enough and applied some more red lipstick. I was conscious that Lucy Westenra needed to look older than my own 24 years. I'd done the screen test and was immediately told that I'd got the part. After dancing around my hotel room for 24 hours I'd come down to earth with a bang. Mr Coppola wanted me to stay at his house and remain in character – and now here I was waiting for a limo to take me there.

'*IIIIIII'm* Lucy Westenra,' I said again to my reflection, trying to exude breathy sexual confidence, but instead all I managed to do was steam up the mirror. Nothing was working and my confidence was under the floor, my breasts were limp sacks and I wanted to go home. Suddenly, standing in the ladies' room at the Beverly Hills Hotel didn't seem as exciting as it was meant to be. I thought about my tiny baby at home in London and got a knot in my stomach, so I finished my make-up hastily, resolving to quickly call Gary before the limo arrived. I left the bathroom with one more 'I'm Lucy Westenra' and dashed to the payphones in the lobby.

As I picked up the phone I remembered the time difference and my heart fell. I knew that, despite the fact that Gary would be out here to join me soon enough, I'd prefer to be at home and between the sheets with him. I replaced the phone and looked around the big, airy lobby, inhabited by lots of old, powerful-looking people with toned bodies and dark tans. I felt very young and pale, lost in a very big town. A cloud of darkness rolled over me like a sickness in the pit of my stomach and I wanted to bolt to LAX and grab the next flight back to London. The ache in my stomach and the blackness in my mind were not supposed to be there. This was supposed to be my big break, a break worth leaving my baby and new husband for. I left the booth and made my way across the lobby, trying to dodge the cloud that pursued me. Out in the blinding sun I was flagged down by a bellboy who was loading my luggage into a waiting limousine.

'Mrs Kemp, I presume?' he said, opening the door of the limo a sliver, as if he approved of my outfit: the black cocktail dress with large shoulder pads that accentuated my curvy figure, the high heels and the slightly slutty make-up. I realised this was my last chance to pull myself together and I raised my chin and kept my gaze steady.

'No,' I replied, lips set in a bumptious pout, '*I'm* Lucy Westenra.'

The limo sped along Sunset Boulevard and out of town.

LOVE AND MARRIAGE

Soon we hit the coast highway and were winding our way through rocky terrain. The houses around us became further and further apart, and ever grander. I opened my pocket mirror and checked my appearance one more time, deciding to tie a red scarf around my neck for a bit of decadent glamour.

Who are you trying to kid, Sadie? You are leaking milk, your bra is stuffed with socks, you've just had a baby and you're stomach is fleshy and you're carrying too many extra pounds. Lucy Westenra? More like a plain young mum from Camden Town.

I shrank back into the leather seat of the limo and listened to the voice in my head. Who was I trying to kid? Suddenly we turned off the highway and climbed inland, entering a lush green valley. We passed a sign saying 'Napa Valley', which didn't mean anything to me apart from 'too far from home'. After another half-hour of passing through vineyards and scrubland, we slowed to a stop outside a pair of huge gates. Without the driver having to speak the gates opened and we rolled along a sweeping drive, coming to rest outside a massive, sprawling house.

I swallowed hard and gathered my belongings together, dropping my pocket mirror and lipstick as I did so. I put on my Ray-Bans and high heels and stepped out of the car. There in front of me was Francis Ford Coppola, who grabbed me around the waist and hugged me close.

'Hello,' I said, staring him straight in the eye, 'I'm Lucy Westenra.'

Francis winked and squeezed my waist and I prayed that he didn't feel the excess baby fat there. If he did, he appeared to like it.

'Welcome to my home,' he said, leading the way up the steps to the house. 'Treat the place as if it was your own.'

A maid followed us with my luggage and shut the door on the outside world, locking me inside Francis's instead. He led me through to a large, salon-type room and there lolling on a sofa were a man and a woman getting intimate with each other.

'Now, Lucy, do you know these two?'

Of course I knew Winona Ryder, world-famous movie star, and Gary Oldman, one of the most extraordinarily talented English actors of his generation. But this was not the time to be impressed by them, or even to call them by their own names since we were supposed to be doing everything 'in character' as preparation for the movie.

'Hello,' I greeted them coquettishly, lighting a cigarette. 'I'm charmed. And I'd love a drink.'

Francis poured us all a drink and left me alone with them.

'You three get to know each other,' he said with a backward glance as he departed. 'And Lucy,' he added, coming back to give me another hug, 'there's a hairdresser coming in half an hour to give you a snip, OK?'

Winona dragged me to the sofa to sit between her and Gary, and there I stayed, smoking and downing my martini as quickly as possible. The alcohol tasted disgusting, and I wasn't used to its powerful effect. Until

LOVE AND MARRIAGE

two days before I'd been drinking orange juice from Safeway so as not to pollute my breast milk. I dismissed the thought, because now I was in Napa Valley with Francis Ford Coppola.

Stop thinking, Sadie! Leave Sadie behind. Lucy wouldn't miss her kid and her husband – she'd use the excuse that she was away from him to party and flirt and…

'So, Lucy, are you married?' said Winona conspiratorially.

'Yes,' I replied, draining my martini and looking Gary dead in the eye, 'but that doesn't mean I'm not looking for some fun.'

Winona laughed and Gary winked before getting up to make me another martini.

The room began to spin slightly and I felt the need to find a bathroom and compose myself. Leaving the other two, I ventured out to find one, listening to my echoing footsteps.

'Are you OK, Ms Westenra?' said a young woman who had appeared as if from nowhere. 'I'm Mr Coppola's assistant.'

'The bathroom?' I managed to say without slurring, and she smiled and showed me where to go.

'By the way, Lucy, the hairdresser has arrived for you,' she added, holding open a door.

'Thank you, but I won't be needing him. My hair is how I like it,' I said quickly, not wanting anyone to touch my newly styled hair. The woman's expression didn't change, as if she had been expecting this response.

'Oh, but it's not the hair on your head he's here to style,' she said, pointing downwards. 'Because of the nude scenes the studio require you to be styled a certain way and he knows that in England the ladies don't shave and clip ... *down there*, but over here we need to keep it small and tidy.'

I locked myself in the bathroom and digested this news. Then I inspected my full hair growth 'down there'. I was shocked to think that anyone would want it any other way than the way it was – natural. In London in those days, people didn't mess about with it at all. Suddenly I felt embarrassed by my natural growth. It seemed like another thing that I had got wrong. The martini was blurring my vision and making me feel dizzy. I gripped the basin, knowing I had to go back to the lounge and continue to be Lucy Westenra. But I knew I wasn't her, not really. Yes, maybe with the booze and the good-looking movie stars, but was I up to it?

Pull yourself together and get back out there... You've got a role in a Francis Ford Coppola movie and if he wants you to live in character, then you goddamn well do it, if he wants you to jump, you jump, and if he wants you to shave your tush, you just do it.

I knew the voice in my head was right but I felt like a fraud. I felt like I'd convinced Francis that I was like Lucy Westenra, that I was a sexual vixen, a party girl with no morals who would sleep with anyone's husband. I'd done this because I wanted the part. Every actress in the world had gone for that part and I'd got it. This was potentially the start of something massive in my career, a role that would launch me in major-league Hollywood.

The only problem was, I couldn't shake the feeling that I had betrayed Francis, who had treated me like a surrogate daughter, taken me into his house, and that really I was just shy Sadie who felt as if she was the most unattractive woman in the world.

So – stop feeling like this. It's easy. Sadie is dead and from now on you have to be brutal and do whatever it takes to break Hollywood. This is your time, girl – live the dream.

I unlocked the door to the bathroom with new resolve. Fuck it. This was the dream indeed, and any woman would be crazy not to live it to the full.

And so I did. The filming of *Bram Stoker's Dracula* passed in a whirl of parties and attention. I erased my mumsy past and although I thought about Fin every day I forced myself to concentrate on the filming. It wasn't hard because hanging out with Gary Oldman was seductive too. We ate in the Chateau Marmont, the hotel famous for the death there of *The Blues Brothers* star John Belushi. Gary and Fin had arrived in LA and we had set up home. Gary had even landed himself in a major movie called *The Bodyguard* with Whitney Houston. In every way we were living the life of Riley and being invited to all the best parties.

All the while Gary was doing most of the work of holding the family together but I could tell he was scared that he was losing me to this glamorous world. I assured him that he wasn't but it seemed like the more worried he became, the more smothered I felt. Things were finally happening for me; the little scruff urchin who'd been on free school meals was now grown up, in Hollywood, filming with Coppola. All those dreams imagined under the duvet in some council flat or other for so many years were coming true. The more Gary clung on to me, the more I felt like pushing him away, because it began to remind me of my dad, when he suffocated me with love as a child and I always ran away.

Meanwhile in Hollywood my new agent, Josh Lieberman, lined up more screen tests and scripts for me.

'You're hot at the moment, Sadie. This is the time to stay in LA and capitalise on the success of *Dracula*,' he told me.

'But what about my son? Gary and I live in London. We can't move here permanently.'

'So what? This is your time, Sadie,' said Josh meaningfully. 'Don't blow it.'

At the same time I'd been sent a script from London for a low-budget movie called *Shopping*. While I was partying and wrestling with my conscience in Los Angeles, I read the script and the story captured my imagination. The next morning I called Gary, who was back in London, and told him I was coming home. The next call I made was to Josh Lieberman.

LOVE AND MARRIAGE

'I'm going back to London,' I said definitely, holding my breath.

'What the fuck for?'

'I want to do this film called *Shopping*.'

'What the fuck? Some tinpot squeaky film with no budget? You're committing career suicide, Sadie,' he said before signing off.

On the plane home I watched the clouds disappear below me. It was time – I was homesick – and despite the feeling that I was perhaps throwing away my career success at its peak, I felt compelled to go home and do this film. It was a typical Sadie thing to do: just when things were going well, run away. At the same time the right thing was to get back home to my reality and my life with Gary. But, as I suspected, reality was never my strong point and falling back into the routine of being a wife and mother the way that Gary wanted wasn't working. I felt that I was letting him down. He was so intellectual and well-read, and although he was always helping me improve my reading and sophistication, I always felt out of my depth with him.

Soon I met up with the director of *Shopping*, Paul Anderson. He told me that they wanted to use an unknown male actor for the lead and he wanted to take me to a play so I could check out this young actor. Coincidentally it happened that Philip Ridley, a friend of mine who had written *The Krays*, had also written this play, *The Fastest Clock In The Universe*, and the actor was called Jude Law.

I arranged to meet Philip at the theatre so I could watch this actor.

As I waited for Philip in the foyer before the show I saw a sallow, blond youth leaning against a wall chatting to a friend. He was thin and gangly and couldn't have been older than 19. Philip grabbed my hand and led me towards the young man.

'Sadie, I wanted you to meet Jude Law,' he said hurriedly, leaving the two of us together while he went to the bar. I smiled at this Jude, who offered a shy smile and a hand in return. I suddenly felt my 25 years, a married woman with a child. Something about him made me extremely nervous and I blushed.

The next week I sat in a dingy rehearsal room in east London waiting to do the screen test for *Shopping*. Across from me, Jude sat astride a chair and waited pensively. The silence between us crackled and I couldn't help but watch him surreptitiously. After the test, as I left the room, I felt like an incredibly heavy weight was pressing down on my heart and squeezing it. I tried to cut the weight loose but I couldn't. It was an unshakeable premonition and an unwelcome one – like being confronted with the juicy apple in the Garden of Eden. I felt that it was my fate to spend the rest of my life with Jude.

Loneliness sits on me heavy and hard.
Like a blanket of cream
Penetrating every inch,
Every pore.
It whirls around my head –
Intoxicating and real, stuttering
Voices that say, 'come on'
'don't give up', 'keep going',
'you can'.
I smile to myself at the pure
Imperfection –
A girl grown up – lost in reflection –
In love, in sadness, in life's drunkenness
I flew like a moth round each burning candle.
My little wing singed, slow to amble.

CHAPTER SEVEN
Big Changes

It was 1992 and the rave culture that had engulfed the country was being replaced by an upsurge of guitar-led Grunge bands like Nirvana, whose hit 'Smells Like Teen Spirit' provided the perfect soundtrack as the economy slipped into recession. People had no money and in London there was a feeling of gloom.

Against this backdrop I got the part for *Shopping*, starring opposite Jude, and filming began. I knew that Gary was as devoted as ever and I understood that by even entertaining thoughts of Jude, I was jeopardising an idyllic home life, the most secure and wonderful relationship I'd ever had. I crushed all unwelcome ideas about this new man and focused on the filming, but it wasn't as easy as that. Jude was there, and I saw how I was beginning to prefer this straightforward young man to the ultra-intellectual older husband who, not by his own choice but simply by being himself, made me feel a little inferior. Still,

I rejected all my dark thoughts, but soon it became clear that Jude was also interested in me.

On a night shoot we were sitting side by side in a car (I was playing Jo, a spunky Irish girl; Jude was playing Billy, a gangly cockney youth), while outside crew members ran about setting up stunts. Smoke was billowing around the car and lights were being rigged, then altered, filters added or taken away. Inside the car it was almost painful for me to sit next to him, so powerful was this force I felt drawing me to him. I tried to concentrate on the crew outside the car, convincing myself that it was all in my mind, that whatever I felt was not reciprocated by him. Then he turned to look at me, his stare intense and hungry. I allowed my gaze to take him in as his almond-shaped, avocado-green eyes thundered their way into my soul. His head was shaved and he was wearing tight black trousers, styled in a way that was distinctly Brandoesque.

Time slowed down as we were intensely trapped inside our bubble in the car and I realised we were destined to be together.

'Cut!' shouted the director from the set and almost immediately we snapped out of our bubble and rejoined the real world.

After that we started to spend all our time together between shots, hanging out in my caravan, which I decorated to look like my own boudoir, and Jude brought Hendrix to put on the tape player as well as introducing me to a new band from Bristol called Massive Attack. He also had a demo from a band featuring two brothers from Manchester who he said were called the Gallaghers. He would chain-smoke and fix his mischievous eyes on me and loaf around with his rangy arms and legs dangling. He was very thin and hadn't fully grown into his adult body. He seemed to throw on clothes that often colour-clashed, because he was colour blind. His easy charm and calm were a breath of fresh air when I thought about Gary's controlled power-dressing and artistic influences.

The more I felt for Jude, the more guilt I felt, and I tried to fix things with Gary. We started to have disagreements and the more we argued, the more I felt that I needed space to myself, to figure out where things were going wrong. I couldn't be logical about the attraction to Jude. It was like the 'paradise syndrome': I had it all – the career and the perfect family – but I felt that I had to destroy whatever was good before someone else took it away from me. I told Gary that I needed to separate for a while to sort out my feelings. Filming for *Shopping* finished and I moved out of Gary's house with Fin and just a suitcase. There was no real fighting. Gary was too grown-up to try to resolve our differences like that, and maybe hoped the separation was only temporary. I hoped so too, but underneath I knew I was on a different course. I couldn't get Jude out of my head, so we agreed to take a holiday together, in Bali. Up to that point nothing physical had happened between us and I was keen that we should have separate rooms and also asked Zoe to come with us, to emphasise that we were still just friends. Once we were in Bali, we couldn't hide our feelings from each other or Zoe and the relationship began.

Exploring the magical island of Bali, with its exotic smells and ancient temples, brought Jude and I even closer and gradually we realised that we had no choice but to be together, so I made my decision.

Zoe and I found a flat to share in Primrose Hill. It wasn't a glamorous place but we could move in straight away and I was desperate to keep some stability for Fin. I was starting all over again with just a suitcase and an overwhelming love for a boy I barely knew. It was the force of this love and the fact that Jude was intensely ambitious that made me feel out of control. And because I had my own career too, from the very beginning we were often apart. Sometimes circumstances seemed to conspire against us. I saw that it was not going to be a relationship that I could control and already it felt overwhelming. It was very different from the relationships I'd had with Lucien and Gary and even with my father. In those relationships, love came almost too easily. This time it felt perfect, and that scared the life out of me.

I had enough money but I wasn't rich and had to be careful. Still, compared with Jude, who was still living hand-to-mouth between acting jobs, I was wealthy. I'd lend him cash for his bus fare or to pay his bills if he was really stuck. After watching him work on the set of *Shopping* I knew that he was incredibly serious about the craft of

BIG CHANGES

acting and studied intensely to perfect whatever role he was playing. Almost immediately he got offered a role in Cocteau's play *Les Parents Terribles*, which would later – retitled *Indiscretions* – transfer from the West End to Broadway. This meant that he would be away in the States for nine months. We promised each other our commitment and to protect our perfect love, but I waved him off with a feeling of immense trepidation. Once he had left, I immediately looked around me for something new, something close to home, to occupy me and help me to re-find myself, a self that was lost to this new love. It was mad, but even early on in the relationship I was always looking for a way to burst the bubble and reject him before he could take his love away. It was a way of rebelling against the fear I felt. I needed a distraction, a new identity – something for me.

I found it in Indie music. There was an air of excitement in London about a clutch of talented guitar bands like Pulp. The recession was ending and things were looking more dynamic in pop culture. Zoe started going out with Steve Mackey, Pulp's bass player. In 1994 she and I started to hang out with the band and I felt as if I was at the cutting edge again. I was introduced to their lead singer, Jarvis Cocker, and Antony Genn, another musician in the band. I felt I was back at the heart of the hip music scene – well, if not the centre, on the outskirts. I was ready for the fun that I felt I'd missed out on in my early twenties. Antony introduced me to Justine Frischmann and the other members of Elastica. I also met her cohort and muse Brett Anderson, lead singer of the hottest band on the block, Suede. I was nervous and stuttering in front of all these musos, as they were by far the coolest and most talented I'd ever met. Justine was the leader of a hot group of female musicians who were tough and androgynous and fought the girls' corner and they gave me a mission while Jude was away in New York.

I was nervous waiting for him to get home from the airport when he finally finished the play in New York. How would we feel about each other? Would the passion still be there? I needn't have worried and we took up where we'd left off. His reputation as an actor was growing, but when I introduced him to all my new crowd he was quickly at home.

I decided to sell my old flat in West Hampstead, which had been rented out since before I moved in with Gary, and with the proceeds I bought a house in Chamberlain Street in Primrose Hill, and Jude moved in. It was 1995 and Blur and Oasis were never far from the jukebox at our local in Camden Town or on the CD player. Jude had introduced me a few years earlier to his acting crowd, people like Johnny Lee Miller and Ewan McGregor. These two were filming *Trainspotting*, which was about heroin addiction, and all my friends' bands – Pulp, Elastica and Blur – were doing numbers for the soundtrack. Our life settled down and Jude was great with Fin, while things between Gary and I were amicable. We had a nice social scene with Sean

BIG CHANGES

Pertwee, Johnny Lee Miller and Ewan McGregor, and the group of us set up our own film company, Natural Nylon. Jude had introduced me to his parents, retired teachers who lived in France. I'd been worried about meeting them, what with being the 'older woman' and having a child from another marriage, but they welcomed me immediately into the family and made me feel comfortable.

Meanwhile I was looking around for the next step in my career, but being in love meant that I wasn't feeling any urge to push things. Then Steve from Pulp called me and asked me to be in their new video and I nearly fell over myself to say yes. Forget Francis Ford Coppola, I was more nervous about being in a Pulp video. It was a track called 'Common People' and they wanted me to play a posh woman, idealised in the lyrics. I tried to tell Jarvis that I was just as common as they all were but they just laughed and told me to get on with it. The shoot day was great fun and the video was soaked in bright colours and retro quirky clothes. It became an iconic image of the times and an important part of Britpop history.

In this period, when Jude was off being creative and Natural Nylon was also keeping him busy, I wanted something creative for myself. Jemima French and I would sit on Primrose Hill talking about how we both dreamed of designing clothes and wanted to connect with our femininity. Working together would be the perfect antidote to the macho meetings around the table at Natural Nylon. We decided that we would start small, with a range of underwear that appealed to the senses. At once we started writing down ideas, and these spawned proper meetings and drawings. We had knickers that smelt of lavender, or adorned with cats that would purr when stroked. Some of our underwear had secret pockets for keepsafes. What started as a hobby grew quickly and we started to plan our first commercial collection.

Trainspotting was released in 1996. There was a frenzy in the media around this new film, which was rumoured to be the best British movie for a generation. Jude and I went up to Edinburgh for the opening party, which was held in an old stone tenement that had been glamorously decorated for the occasion. All the gang were there, along with the movie's stars, Johnny Lee Miller and Ewan McGregor. The rooms and stairs were packed with actors and celebrities toasting the film with champagne, everyone lost in the buzz of the moment.

Zoe called me there and I searched through my handbag for my mobile.

'Sadie, darling, I've worked out your dates and you must be ovulating. If you want to join me and get pregnant, tonight's the night.'

A couple of weeks later I was throwing up violently. A pee test revealed that I was pregnant. Jude and I discussed it and were both thrilled, but my own euphoria was dented by an almost immediate and overwhelming urge to throw up. Within hours I was vomiting so violently that I was taken to the Hospital of St John &

BIG CHANGES

St Elizabeth in St John's Wood. They put me on a drip and told me that I was so dehydrated I'd have to stay there for a week. Then the doctor told me that I would have to rest for the entire pregnancy as things were looking complicated. I was disappointed that something so wonderful could make me feel so ill, especially after Fin had been such an easy pregnancy. Now I was confined to my bed, couldn't eat or even contemplate going near a restaurant and Jude was away a lot, working hard, although he was devoted and supportive when he was at home. I had a nagging sense that I was jeopardising my love. Jude was out there, his star was rising, and I was sitting on the sofa, getting fatter and chewing Hubba Bubba gum – the only thing I could stomach. A day would seem like ten years while I waited for Jude to come back. Meanwhile, Zoe had given birth already to a son, Marley, and was breastfeeding him while I rolled around on the floor rubbing my stomach with every cream available.

'I can't dooooo this any mooooooore,' I said, anointing my vast belly with avocado, cocoa butter and tea oil.

'Oh, stop complaining,' said Zoe, while Marley slept at her breast. 'Look what you get at the end of it.' At that moment Marley woke and puked all over her. The two of us fell about laughing. It was all I could do to stop myself crying.

I kept myself positive by preparing for the birth, buying baby clothes and getting all the stuff ready for the baby. I decorated the house in bright colours – red, orange and purple, a psychedelic homage to my father's art. Zoe and I waddled down to Camden Town to buy some clothes and on the way I started to feel distinctly strange.

'I think I'll go home now,' I said, feeling like something was happening inside.

'I'll come with you,' Zoe replied, looking concerned.

'No, I want to be alone,' I said, smiling and rubbing my stomach. At home I curled up in a ball and waited. When Jude got back I looked up at him and said, 'I think the baby is coming,' at which he looked worried.

'No, it's much too early – you're only 33 weeks,' he said.

'I know, but I think we'd better go to the hospital anyway.'

We got there and the midwife took one look at me and pointed to the exit.

'Go home and rest,' she said. 'You aren't in labour, love.'

'Could you just check me anyway?' I pleaded, remembering Fin and having visions of delivering in the taxi on the way home. They gave me a scan and told me that everything was fine, but as we left the hospital my waters broke. Jude went white and we were rushed upstairs. Seven hours later, on 3 October 1996, Rafferty Jellicoe was born, looking exactly like a Pre-Raphaelite cherub. It had been exactly the same length of labour as Fin. Instantly the sickness that had dogged me through the entire pregnancy faded away. Now I was able to enjoy a glass of champagne and as much soft cheese as I wanted. It was idyllic to be in a private room with my baby in a cot and Jude next to me,

BIG CHANGES

as fathers were allowed to spend the night. We felt as if the world was perfect.

Unfortunately, Jude was shooting *Wilde* with Stephen Fry and had to go back to work the very next morning. Because Rafferty had come so early, Jude had no choice but to finish the movie, so couldn't be with me in the first few weeks. Once back home, I didn't want a nanny as I wanted to be alone with Raff, but I had a sense of growing unease, like the low that dogged me with Fin, pulling me down for no reason. Jude was the devoted father, coming home after work and cooking dinner for me and looking after Raff. We all slept in the same bed, and I was beginning to feel a security I'd never felt before with Jude.

We took Raff and Fin to Ludlow to see my mother, who now had an ever more settled family life with Holly and Jade, and with the girls' grandparents nearby. Naturally Holly and Jade loved looking after Raff and Fin and we all had a wonderful time. Mum and I had grown really close now that I had matured into a woman, and we could see eye to eye. Yet this only made me feel like I was failing in my relationship with my father.

Dad's behaviour was growing more erratic. That same year he had climbed on to the roof of his house in Ashton and been arrested for throwing things on to the street below and trying to start a riot. He ended up in Strangeways Prison and I got a desperate call from him, asking me for help. After a couple of weeks inside, he was granted bail. Once he was out, I offered to lend him some money. I felt that the best thing would be for him to leave the country and go somewhere tranquil, where he could get some peace of mind. A friend of mine drove him to the airport, handed him a wad of cash and put him on a plane for Bali. I was worried because doing this meant that he had broken his bail conditions, but in a way I was pleased that he was getting away and hoped it would help his mental state. Two days later I got a phone call.

'Is that Sadie?' said a strange female voice in a German accent.

'Yeah, who's that?'

'I'm with your father here in Munich.'

'Munich?'

'Yah, he is here in the airport. He has no money. He is trying to come home.'

I was furious with Dad, and organised a ticket to get him home. When he got back he explained that he was ill. I didn't believe him – all I saw was a sad, pathetic man, a man who had wasted his talent.

When he got back to Manchester he was diagnosed with hepatitis C. The depression that had pursued him all these years, the psychosis and the bad trips all seemed to catch up with him and he slid into madness. He would go into the supermarket in his pyjamas and, not having any money, he'd eat what he could in the aisles. Anne had left him, so he was alone in the squalor of his house in Mossley Road. As for me, I couldn't bear to think about it. I didn't want him ruining my life again and couldn't risk this happening, so I had to shut him out and concentrate on me and my new family.

By now I was feeling low and lost with my little baby and Jude out working all the time. Eventually I wanted to press the self-destruct button. I arranged a babysitter for Raff and Fin and went out. I partied all night to let off steam and when I got home the next day I was racked with guilt. How could I act in this way when I had such a beautiful life? It didn't make any sense. I was sitting at my dressing table, not feeling anything – just numb. Nothing seemed to make sense. I felt as if I was leaving my body as I watched my arm slowly pick up a pair of scissors. It was if I was being sucked down lower into the chair and the scissors seemed be drawn to my arm. I appeared to have cut myself. Time seemed to stand still as the blood dripped down my arm. There was no sense of panic within me – I just felt empty.

When I managed to pull my thoughts together, I picked up the phone and called a friend.

'I think I need help,' I whispered. 'Meet me at the bridge in Primrose Hill.'

I walked to the railway bridge that my father had painted red so many years earlier, when I was a toddler. A bridge that seemed to embody the journey back and forth between my old pain and future hopes. I looked at the cuts on my arm and wept – why, I didn't know. I had everything I wanted but my power of reasoning had deserted me. My friend arrived and took me to a doctor who organised for me to be admitted to the Nightingale Hospital in Marylebone, where I was diagnosed with severe postnatal depression. It was a relief, in a way, to be in hospital, a place I'd always felt safe. They gave me some medication to treat the depression and all of its raging symptoms.

The drugs did work and as soon as I had a proper diagnosis I felt like my old self. It was as if a veil was lifted from my eyes. I hadn't realised that I'd been suffering from PND with Fin as well, but after the doctors told me how common the condition was I could see it for what it was and felt immense relief. Life with Raff and Fin became happy once more and Jude and I decided to get married. We didn't want a huge wedding, and felt that a local village fête-type ceremony in a barge on the banks of the canal in nearby Little Venice was the perfect way to celebrate our life together. I still couldn't believe that I was about to marry the love of my life and, with my capacity for conjuring up the worse-case scenario, didn't buy a dress because I didn't want to jinx it. Johnny Lee Miller was to be Jude's best man and in August 1997, a few weeks before the wedding, he came to the house to have a drink. He stuck his head round the door and I saw he had a girl with him, a very beautiful girl that I'd never met but recognised all the same.

'Hello,' the girl said. 'I'm Kate.' It was Kate Moss. She sat down at the kitchen table, lit a cigarette and made herself totally at home. 'You must be soooo excited to be getting married!' she said with a smile that made her eyes shine like diamonds. Already I knew her face so well as she was one of the world's most fêted models, but when I met her I loved her straight away, even though we were strangers. She had this aura that just followed her, as if the room she entered was suddenly full of her presence. She also had a mischievous look in her eye and I knew I'd found a soul mate. Jude, Johnny, Kate and I sat in the basement kitchen and chatted for hours. Our huge wooden table and comfortable benches usually encouraged people to relax and be social. After a few hours of wine and food Kate was singing and dancing with abandon. I couldn't help but be disarmed by her.

'What you wearing to the wedding then, sweetheart?' she asked, standing up and grabbing my arm as if to tug me off to my closet.

'Oh, er, well, I dunno yet.'

'You what? Are you mad?' She looked at me as if I'd committed a crime, before getting on her mobile and calling someone. In a few minutes she'd arranged for me to go round to her house and try on a dress. A few days later I was once again in her clutches and was trying on the dress that John Galliano had made for her twenty-first birthday.

'You can borrow it,' she said, smiling. 'It fits you perfectly.'

The dress was beautiful, cut on the bias and with a fishtail finish. I was overcome by her generosity and maternal instinct. Like me she had a free spirit, a crazy need to express herself, but as well she was a loyal person with a good heart.

September arrived and so did the day of the wedding. We had decorated the wedding barge and an area around it with bunting, ballons and English traditional fare. By the time I stood beside Jude I finally accepted that we were going to be married. My dream had come true and nothing now could come between us. Apart from the dress, I was barefoot and without make-up, wanting nothing fake to destroy the beauty of the day. The reception was attended by close friends like Zoe and Jemima and those bright young things of British film, Johnny Lee Miller and Sean Pertwee. It was relaxed and informal and the kids ran around barefoot; no one had a care in the world. All my family and grandparents were there, and Jude's too. I'd even managed to smooth over my relationship with my father and he was there on his best behaviour, along with Anne and my half-brothers.

We took a penthouse suite at the Covent Garden Hotel which had just opened. We were followed there by our friends and the wedding celebrations continued.

Many holidays and parties followed with our north London gang and life was a constant social whirl. FrostFrench had manufactured its first line of underwear and now had other pieces in its collection. We held a show at the St Martins Lane hotel, or rather it was more of an art installation which featured a 16-year-old girl in bed with a young beau. We'd torn the room out and put in goldfish

BIG CHANGES

tanks, a cat, a record player and other clutter. All my friends and colleagues were there, including some prestigious fashion editors and the wonderfully talented, now sadly late, Alexander McQueen. To have him there, the king of fashion, meant a lot. We followed this up with a show at the Duke of York's Theatre called *GIRL*, which I wrote up like a play. Jude's sister, Tash Law, made the backdrop and Kate opened the show, modelling and dressing behind a screen playing the role of Cool Girl, then Rose Ferguson was Rock Girl and Leah Wood was Soul Girl and my sister Holly was Book Girl. The London glitterati turned out in force, including the fashion photographer Mario Testino, and it was followed by an all-night party. The trouble was that neither Jemima nor I realised how much time and effort went into running a business and we both had small children. As our success grew we both became stressed and our creative disagreements often ended in screaming arguments, and on one occasion a punch-up. When it was over we both stood back and laughed at our stupidity, the two of us looking like Pats and Eddie in *Absolutely Fabulous* tearing each other's hair out over a swatch of knicker fabric.

The partying and the stress of the business took a toll on my relationship with Jude. I had managed to keep my career going, working on projects such as *Final Cut*, *Love, Honour and Obey* and *Uprising*. The more in demand Jude was professionally, the more of a drama queen I became. As he matured into a man and had more responsibilities, I started to act like a child and a lot of the time we were living on a knife edge, but we made it work because of Rafferty and because we knew that what we had was worth the effort. Soon Jude had completed *The Talented Mr Ripley* and was finishing up filming *An Enemy at the Gates* in Berlin. It was just as he returned that I found out I was pregnant again. It was a wonderful moment to have my husband and my two sons and now hopefully one more child to complete our family. But once again he landed another film immediately. This time it was Stephen Spielberg's new movie, *A.I.*, and it was not something he could turn down. It meant six months in Hollywood and a house in Malibu.

So we upped sticks and moved to LA, where our house overlooked the ocean and was picture-perfect. I was already a few months through pregnancy and realised that this move meant having the baby in LA, so we registered with Santa Monica Hospital in Hollywood. Life looked heavenly. I settled into Malibu and watched the dolphins go by with Fin and Raff while Jude started filming, and things were once again perfect. Towards the end of my gestation we invited some of the gang out from England to stay because the singer-songwriter and later fashion designer Pearl Lowe's boyfriend's band, Supergrass, were playing a huge gig with Radiohead in LA. We had a guest house that was separate from the main house and Pearl, Danny, Kate and Meg Matthews all stayed there. I still had seven weeks to go until my due date and so I thought it was safe to organise a dinner

BIG CHANGES

after the concert where I intended to do a bit of matchmaking for Kate, by introducing her to an actor friend of Jude's. A stretch limousine arrived to pick us all up and take us downtown to the concert and we were all singing as we went. As we stood watching the gig I started to feel strange. It was like a compression on my lower back, and my spine was throbbing. I totted up how many weeks pregnant I was and came up with 33. I put any doubts about the wisdom of my organising the dinner to the back of my mind. It was great to see friends from home and nothing was going to spoil the evening. My sister Holly and her boyfriend Ben, who I'd also invited over for the gig, stood next to me as I had a sudden twinge and grabbed her for support.

'Are you all right?' said Holly, wrinkling her brow.

'Fine. I just feel a bit weird. I think I might be going into labour.'

'But you're only 33 weeks – you *can't* be.'

Holly looked at me doubtfully but I turned away, convincing myself that what I was feeling weren't labour pains. After the gig we all sat down to dinner and Kate's blind date still hadn't turned up. Meanwhile, deep inside me, the contractions were coming more regularly.

'Hold on … hold on…' I whispered to myself, not prepared to allow the truth to enter my head.

Holly kept looking over at me as I got whiter and whiter and occasionally gripped the table. At this point I was finding it hard to conceal my discomfort any more.

'What's the matter, hon?' said Kate, clearly concerned.

'Oh, nothing,' I insisted, while madly ringing her blind date on my mobile, trying to find out his whereabouts, while literally keeping my legs crossed and willing the contractions away. I cursed my body. How could this be happening again? I told Jude that I was having contractions and he didn't believe it was possible. Soon Holly was timing them as coming every five minutes.

'Sadie, I think we need to go to the hospital,' she said.

'Just give me five more minutes for this guy to turn up.'

'No, now. Let's go,' said Holly firmly, and she and Jude helped me to the waiting limo, with Kate rushing in at the last minute, determined to be with me at the birth. As we headed toward Santa Monica, Kate spotted a convenience store.

'Stop!' she shouted to the driver. 'We're going to need supplies.'

The limo stopped and the others dived out quickly to buy champagne and cigarettes before rushing on to the hospital, where, outside the emergency department, a nurse was waiting for me with a wheelchair. As soon as we got upstairs the midwife took one look at me and said, 'You're not in labour.'

I rolled my eyes: it was like Groundhog Day all over again. I got out of the wheelchair and walked around on my tiptoes in the examination room, as a way of relieving the pressure on my spine.

'I *am* in bloody labour,' I said through gritted teeth. 'Can you please just examine me?'

The midwife went off to get a doctor and left us behind

BIG CHANGES

a curtain in the examination room. Despite my agitated state I had my friends with me and entertained them by doing the cancan behind the curtain, pulling it back and forth like a skirt. Kate got up and joined me and we managed to ease the stress of the situation by laughing at me leaping about with my huge bump. Soon the midwife returned and examined me.

'OK, ma'am,' she said, admitting her mistake. 'You are five centimetres dilated.'

I smiled with relief as we could finally get under way. Jude put some Bob Marley on and sat and ate bananas because he was so nervous, while Holly and Kate paced about the hall. Almost seven hours later, on 25 October 2000, a baby girl was born, weighing only four pounds and eleven ounces. She was all lips and squidge. We were disarmed by our little bundle of joy. Kate and Holly reappeared holding a huge bunch of irises and Jude and I, who hadn't yet fixed on a name, decided that she had to be called Iris Tallulah Law.

Because she was so tiny she had to go to an incubator and Jude stayed with me in the hospital while Holly looked after Raff and Fin in Malibu. They kept Iris in for a week so I had to start expressing breast milk to feed her with so that I could go home to be with Raff and Fin and visit her in hospital. The day she came home to Malibu was heaven, as I sat on the deck in the sun breastfeeding her and watching the dolphins play in the water. In my whole lifetime I don't think I've ever felt so complete, surrounded by my three kids, husband and friends who came to admire the new baby.

But illness is cruel and I got that now horribly familiar sinking feeling. I knew that postnatal depression was setting in again. For some reason I'd convinced myself that this time it wouldn't be a problem, that I was on top of it, happy and stable in Malibu. Illness doesn't listen, though, and it was pulling me downwards, seducing me into its cold, dark arms. Jude was trying his hardest to understand and help, but the more we had to socialise at grand dinner parties in Hollywood, the more I felt my self-esteem slipping away. I'd stutter through the evening, feeling like an insignificant shadow. Soon I admitted defeat and went to see a doctor, who diagnosed PND and put me back on medication. I was very scared and constantly checked myself for signs of the madness that afflicted my father. All I could think about was his fate, ending up in a loony bin being treated for psychosis, and I didn't want that to happen to me. The more I worried, the more self-obsessed I became and the less attention I gave to my relationship with Jude, and consequently a distance opened up between us.

Once the filming wrapped we returned to London and life took on a familiar pattern. Time was passing and it seemed that we were endlessly busy with the kids and our careers. Jude was up for lots more roles and I was still feeling low, again struggling to hold the relationship

BIG CHANGES

together, feeling threatened and less than Jude. I hid my pain by falling back on parties and socialising, finding as many distractions as possible. However, I still felt like I was missing something. It was probably a bad idea to get pregnant again, knowing how badly I suffered with both pregnancies and the postnatal blues, but there was part of me that wanted another baby. The intense broodiness I felt was constant. I hoped a new baby would round off our family and bring new happiness. One sunny morning Kate called me.

'Sadie, I'm coming round. I think I'm pregnant.'

'I think I am too,' I said.

Kate came round and we both bought pregnancy tests from Boots and did them together. I was so dehydrated I could barely squeeze out enough pee for the stick. Amazingly we were both with child and we danced around the room.

I knew the pregnancy would be problematic. I was advised to have a stitch to stop the baby being born before 24 weeks and then was confined to bed rest. At the time Jude and I were living in Angier Road in Primrose Hill but had just bought and designed our dream house close by, and were looking forward to its completion. Then Jude got offered a role opposite Nicole Kidman in *Cold Mountain*, directed by Anthony Minghella, and told me that filming was starting in Romania. He was going away again. This was the last thing I wanted and I felt so alone and terrified that my life would unravel. There was nothing I could do except concentrate on keeping my baby well and not going into premature labour again. Luckily I had Kate to keep me company during the pregnancy and I spent my whole time telling her to prepare properly for birth, to have a bag packed and ready and to do all her pelvic floor exercises.

Sure enough, on 33 weeks I felt the ominous pangs of labour. I called Kate immediately.

'What?' she cried. 'You can't be in labour! Stay there – I'm coming round.'

When she arrived I was walking round on tiptoe in the familiar labour dance.

'Where's your bag? We've gotta go, babe,' she said, looking round for my stuff.

'I haven't got it ready yet,' I said, determined to hold off the labour. Jude had just got on a plane to North Carolina to film more of *Cold Mountain* and there was no way I was having the baby without him.

'You haven't got it bloody ready?' Kate shouted. 'After all the earache you've been giving me about being prepared?'

I shrugged apologetically while she ran around stuffing knickers and nightgowns into a plastic bag. She threw me and the bag into her car, a small Jeep that she had on hire at the time. This happened to be followed by about 20 paparazzi who had followed Kate to my house. As we got in the car, with me feeling fat and awful, a photographer stuck a lens in my face.

'Get outta the way!' said Kate, also very pregnant, as

BIG CHANGES

she eased herself into the driving seat. 'We've gotta get to the hospital.'

Obviously the paps followed us all the way and the pains got worse and worse. As I got out of the Jeep at the hospital I dropped my plastic bag full of clothes and knickers spilled out on the road. Another photographer thrust a lens at my face just as I was scooping them up.

'Just leave me alone, can't you!' I shouted, finally snapping as Kate helped me inside.

The doctor who examined me told me that he could give me an injection to put off the labour for a while and I called Jude, who had just landed in the States and had to get a plane straight back again. All my previous births had been natural, without medication, but this time I felt I needed it and requested an epidural to be standing by. It took all my colossal energy to not go into labour until Jude walked in the door after two horrific days of travelling. He'd taken a motorbike from the airport to get him to the hospital faster. When he got there he found some of our friends anxiously waiting: Kate and Jefferson Hack, Rhys Ifans and his girlfriend Jess Morris, as well as Rose Ferguson. The doctors were standing by, telling me that I had five seconds to push the baby out before they intervened and gave me a Caesarean section. With one almighty effort I pushed and out came Rudy, assisted by a plunger that meant he came out with an elongated head, looking like the Bert and Ernie cartoon characters. On 10 September 2002 Rudy Indiana Otis came into the world –

only five-an-a-half pounds, and, like his sister Iris, he had to go into an incubator. In the room, we celebrated by singing the lyrics to the Specials' song 'A Message to You, Rudy' with Kate, Jeff, Rhys and Jess, and Rose, who was to be Rudy's godmother.

Jude left immediately for America and I went home with Rudy. My mother had come to help out with the kids and look after me because she knew I was finding it difficult to cope. I knew that Jude was going almost straight into filming *Cold Mountain* again and I was desperately trying to keep the wave at bay, the wave of depression that I felt could engulf me at any second. It helped that Kate was about to go into labour herself and I was determined to be there for her, as she had been present at the births of my last two children. When I got the call from Jefferson that Kate was having contractions. I got into a Juicy Couture tracksuit and headed to the hospital.

'It's OK, babe, I'm here,' I said, rushing into the delivery room, where Kate was in the first stages of labour. She already had a drip in her arm, and I grabbed her hand and stroked her forehead.

'I've done this four times. I can help you through this,' I reassured her, squeezing her hand hard with the contractions. After a while a nurse tapped me on the shoulder.

'Um, Sadie ... I think you need to let go of her hand.'

'What?' I said, not wanting to be distracted from my task.

'Let go of my bloody hand, Sadie, for God's sake!'

BIG CHANGES

shouted Kate in between labour pains. I looked down and saw that I'd been squeezing it so tight that the blood was shooting back up her drip and interfering with her pain relief. I gave Jefferson an apologetic look and backed away, telling the nurse that I'd rather wait outside. As I paced the corridor I realised my accident-prone streak meant I was a hindrance rather than a help to Kate's birth. Luckily the rest of the birth went OK and Lila was born, a playmate for Rudy.

Soon after, Mum suggested that I have an afternoon off from feeding Rudy and take Rafferty to a children's party that he'd been invited to. It was in Soho and I decided that it would be a way to lift my spirits, so I took Raff and Iris along. The party was being hosted by Pearl, a birthday celebration for her son Alfie. It proved to be a good move as I immediately felt better drinking coffee and chatting away to Pearl's mother and my friend Zoe.

The incidents that took place that afternoon have been well documented in the press but, for legal reasons and out of respect to my family, I'm not going to dwell on them further in the pages of this book. What I will say, though, is that my actions that day were those of a responsible parent who did everything she could to protect her child.

The next morning, I was woken by strange noises in the street outside. It sounded like scaffolding was being erected and I assumed that builders were working out there or the council was digging up the road again. When I peeped through the curtains I couldn't understand what I was seeing. There were four or five news vans with satellite dishes on their roofs and an army of photographers on stepladders all jostling to get the best position to see my house from.

'Oh Christ, what the hell...?' My words trailed off and the possibility dawned on me that this had something to do with the incidents from the day before. I got on the phone to my manager and friends, who all told me that the press had got hold of the story, yet all their 'facts' were wrong. I panicked and didn't know what to do, so I called Jude in and told him what was happening. He was fantastic and understanding, but there was nothing we could do to stop the press running away with a story based on untruths. All of a sudden I was public enemy number one and the criticism cut me wide open, as if I'd been cut with a Stanley knife. I was barely holding it all together anyway. I sat in my kitchen, staggered by the injustice of it all, wearied to the bone of the pressure of my life and wondering what was the point. All I had done was have an afternoon off to take my kids to a birthday party in Soho. From feeling like a good mother, who acted swiftly and responsibly, I now felt like the worst mother in the world for doing nothing other than taking my kids to a party.

The fallout from the incident meant the postnatal depression kicked in even deeper and sent me spiralling downwards. The carpet seemed to come towards me. I stared at a list of things I had to do but all I could see were the specks of hair and fluff on the carpet and how I wanted to pick them all away. There were lots of them but if I kept focusing on the fluff my mind was filled and I couldn't think of anything else. The fluff formed a ball in my hand. Then a voice came from somewhere else in my head, *'Sadie! The list! Come on! The list!'*

I remembered the list and searched the carpet for it vacantly. I was sitting in the middle of my bedroom, my and Jude's room. The large room was dark: I hadn't drawn the curtains for days because they might be out there. Who? Them. The paps. Staring at me, accusing me and lying in wait for another story. The list. I scanned my lovely bedroom in our lovely new house but it felt cold and empty and I couldn't wait to get away from it. Even the chic wallpaper and dark wood furniture seemed to repel me. Jude and I had chosen the house in better days, loving its high ceilings and echoing space. Now it seemed to be moving in towards me. The carpet stretched on for miles and miles in all directions and all I could see was fluff. How was I ever going to pick it all up? I needed to hoover, I needed to get the Hoover...

'Sadie, for fuck's sake, the list!' That voice again, shrill and high-pitched. I remembered why I was searching the carpet. I crawled around on my hands and knees, peering under the four-poster bed for the list. I'd written it on a scrap of paper, and it was a list of everything I needed to do, get and pack. Then I noticed that a bit of paper was tucked into my pocket. I took it out. It was the list that I'd been trying to find for the last 20 minutes. I could have

sworn it was lost. It was there all the time. As I unfolded it, my hands were shaking a little, so I stopped them. Shhhhhhh. Keep it together. On the list was written, 'Things to pack – Rudy's bottles, formula milk, nappies, rash cream, factor 50 suntan lotion, towels, travel cot, cot sheets, babygrows, washing powder...' It went on and on: 'Iris, buy swimsuits, pick up prescriptions, take dogs to kennels, cancel papers, pack travel buggy, buy Raff new trainers, flip-flops, pick up dry cleaning, cancel milk...' On and on...

From somewhere else in the house I heard a loud thump and then a child's scream. It was Iris. She was crying. Then I heard another loud thump and a shout. Rafferty. I knew they were fighting about something but I couldn't move. The list held me frozen. Panic spread across my body like fast ants prickling my skin. The flight was in eight hours' time. We had to leave for the airport in six. I went back to the open suitcase and the mound of kids' clothes I had piled up in it. I'd made the list early that morning, knowing that if I got busy I could get everything done, just.

I started to fold babygrows and pack them neatly, but 15 minutes passed and I realised I was wasting time, so I heaped the rest in. I felt tears in the back of my eyes dribbling towards the front and then they came, cascading down my face and on to the pile of clothes. I collapsed into the suitcase, burying my face in the clothes, as wave after wave of sobbing shook me.

BIG CHANGES

'Sadie?' a voice shouted from somewhere downstairs. 'Do you want toast?'

I picked myself out of the suitcase and ran to the door, wiping my tears. No one was to see me like this. I was OK, just doing the list … holding it together … I was fine.

'No thanks! I'm fine!' I shouted through the open door. I closed it against Rafferty and Iris shouting at each other. I closed it against Zoe, who had come round to see me and was making breakfast. I closed it against the world. The baby monitor crackled into life and I could hear a little whinging noise. Rudy. Oh no … no, no, please … please don't wake up now … not now…

I'd only just put him down and I needed him to sleep. I listened closely with clenched fists. The whinge turned into a cry. One … two … three … four … five…

The bedroom door opened a little. Zoe was trying to come in while balancing two cups of tea and a plate piled with toast. Eventually she managed it by kicking the door with her foot.

'Raff and Iris are going mad with each other downstairs, didn't you hear?'

'Yes,' I said, packing the bottle-sterilising equipment. I had filled the first suitcase. All I had to do now was fill another six.

'And I thought I heard Rudy crying.'

'Its OK, he's stopped. It's all under control.'

Zoe sat on the four-poster bed and ate a piece of toast. My stomach tightened with nausea. Oh, to be able to eat.

I hadn't eaten for weeks, at least not properly since before Rudy was born. Zoe looked at the baby equipment piled up in towers all around me and frowned.

'Are you going to get all that in? I mean, I think you might need a JCB.'

I forced a smile while I struggled to get the zip done up on the first suitcase. Zoe ditched the toast and came to help me but the zip pull broke off and the case burst open, showering babygrows everywhere.

Forward again, the tears marched on like an invading army, just waiting for me to break as I fell to my knees among the debris.

'How am I going to do this? *How* am I meant to *do* everything? *How?*' I shouted at Zoe as she watched open-mouthed. 'How can I pack for myself and four children? *How?*' My breathing quickened and I started to pant. By now I was wringing my hands like a wet rag. Zoe grabbed me and sat me on the bed, saying something, but I couldn't hear her. To me she was moving her lips but not speaking.

'Sadie! Listen to me,' she said. And eventually I heard her, over the screams of my children. 'You need help.'

'What? To pack? I know I do,' I said, returning to the floor.

'No, I mean you need *help*.'

'What shall I do?' I said finally. It was as if a crack had appeared in my shiny façade. Whatever was going wrong between Jude and me, I had put on a united front for the sake of my family. I had made a plan, and that plan had been to have a family holiday in Thailand and mend whatever

BIG CHANGES

was broken. It was just time we needed in order to put things right. Jude was working so hard on *Cold Mountain* and I'd only just had Rudy. We'd been together hardly at all. All we needed was a holiday.

'Well, I don't think you have any choice,' Zoe said, raising an eyebrow in the way she did when it was serious. 'I think you need to go into a clinic.'

'What me? I do? Why?'

'Because I think you're having a breakdown,' she said quietly.

Time stopped. The suitcases spewing clothes became irrelevant. Was it that obvious that I wasn't coping? I got up like a zombie and went to the mirror. My hair was uncut and greasy, my eyes were surrounded by deep black sunken moats and my skin was deathly pale. OK, I'd been a little bit depressed, but I had thought I was coping. Now, it seemed, everyone could see I wasn't. But a clinic? Had it really come to this?

'OK, fine. I will. But I just need to get to Thailand and see Jude,' I protested.

'But you're exhausted, Sadie. You need to rest and…' said Zoe. I cut her off mid-sentence by grabbing a newspaper from the bed and throwing it at her. On the front page was a picture of Jude and a woman sitting very close at some party on the set of the movie and a headline implying something was going on.

'I need to sort this out with him, Zoe. It's probably crap but we need to talk and show a united front.'

Zoe studied the photo and put the paper aside, sighing deeply. I could see by her expression that she didn't care about all that crap. All she cared about was me.

'OK, Sadie, go, but you aren't well enough. It's pretty obvious that you've got postnatal depression again and if you don't get it treated it will get worse.'

Jude and I flew to Thailand separately, at his request, and right away I knew something was wrong. When we met up, I knew that it was over, the way he looked at me. It had gone. I was out of sorts, underweight, depressed and scared. My mother had been worried and urged me not to go but I had ignored her like I ignored Zoe. We got through the holiday, then both of us had to go to LA for a business meeting with our joint agency. When we got to the hotel room I could bear it no longer. I had to have it out with him.

I asked him if he loved me but, really, he didn't need to reply – I knew what the answer would be. The moment had finally arrived and I knew that the relationship with the man I loved was over. That night, the reality of the situation hit home and I realised I could not go on feeling this wretched. I knew I needed support and, thankfully, my American agent called. He immediately came to my rescue, took one look at me in my sorry state and advised me to see a doctor.

I knew that if I was going to have a breakdown I wanted to be at home with my mother and children and not thousands of miles away. I was taken to a clinic and the doctor, a black-haired, hawk-like woman, asked me a series of questions. I didn't like her: she seemed evil, and her room was cluttered with furniture, books and papers. All I wanted was space and peace. She recommended that I enter treatment in an LA clinic straight away. She also insisted on calling me Stacey throughout the assessment.

'No thanks,' I said, getting up from the chair. 'I'll see a doctor when I get home.'

I ran out of the clinic on to La Cienega Boulevard, then walked along in the same direction as the traffic. If I'd taken any of the small alleyways off the sidewalk I could have got away, but as I walked I felt a huge hand wrap around my upper arm from behind.

'Mrs Law, ma'am?' said the massive black guy in the clinic uniform. 'I'm afraid I have to take you back to the clinic.'

'Why?' I said, unable to understand why he wouldn't let go of my arm.

'Under Californian law the patient is not legally allowed to terminate an assessment and therefore I am committing you to our care for 28 days,' he said, turning me and leading me back down the street. Panic rose and engulfed me. It was finally here, the day I'd been dreading all my life. I saw my father standing before me, smiling, as if this was my fate. I was being sectioned, just like he had been, and his madness was inside me. All my worst nightmares came home to roost as if my whole adult life, all the happiness with my man and my children, had been a dream and I'd come straight from childhood to this place.

The psychiatric ward was just as bad as I'd imagined it would be: there were plastic sheets on the bed and bars on the windows. It was quite obvious to me and to the staff that this was not the best place for me. I even took up smoking in order to get out of the ward, as smoking was the only reason you were allowed to leave the building. After all the years of not smoking because of my bad lung, I was driven to it through the full force of my tormented mind. All I needed to do was to get home. I called my family in England, who worked hard on getting me out of there, but it wasn't until a week later that I called Gavin Rossdale, who was living in LA and was allowed to take me to his place in Los Feliz. It was like heaven to suddenly be looked after in an oasis of calm, and soon Zoe arrived from London to accompany me home. I knew that my marriage was over.

The pain is like a broken glass.
Smooth, but sharp and transparent.
Yes my love's all wrong.
It has turned to stone
So I live a life of solitude.

The cracks left me on my own.
Gone were the days we laughed.
Smoking in saloon bars removed
And now it just seems empty and sad,
Bye bye to what we had.

I saw you in a faded dream.
You visited me one more time.
You licked my teeth stained with wine,
But left quickly and took my heart away
So the beat could never start.

CHAPTER EIGHT

Coming Home

As soon as I got back to London I checked myself into a clinic to be treated for my depression but I didn't feel able to open the almighty Pandora's box that was my past. All I needed to carry on was my kids and my work. With this in mind I left the clinic after a week and went back home. The dream house that we'd crafted together was now strangely empty of Jude, who had taken his belongings and rented a place of his own. In order to try and carry on with life, I knew I had to have a distraction. My plan was to conceal my heartbreak from the world by throwing myself into the organisation of a premiere for a film that I had made for FrostFrench. The film featured Helena Christiansen and Jerry Hall and had a circus theme. The screening at Bafta was attended by Kate, Rose Ferguson and Stella McCartney, to name but a few good friends who rallied round to support me, and I made sure I looked as good as could be to face the gathered media.

Even so, just to put one foot in front of the other was like walking over glass, and I bit my lip constantly to provide the adrenalin to get me through that evening.

Of course, the paparazzi and the tabloid media were now camped outside our house and there were daily front-page stories about our marriage breaking up. Leaving the house became a traumatic event, and even taking the children to school had to be planned to the last detail. Did my hair look all right? Were my clothes ironed and respectable? I was dealing with my whole life coming apart and I had to worry about whether there were holes in my tights or how I could put the rubbish out without being seen.

Soon my crisis spread to food. As soon as I sat down to a meal I started to panic. Every single thing I put into my mouth disgusted me. I couldn't eat at all and was losing weight daily. It was as if my mouth itself had become a piece of food and each piece of food was my mouth, so I'd make excuses and leave the table. It was impossible to explain this feeling to my sisters and my mother, who had come to stay with me to help out. In the bathroom mirror I would not see my own face, but my father's, mocking me by saying, '*Sadie, my angel, you know what it's like now, to be me.*'

I put a towel over the mirror, hating myself, what I'd become. I thought back to the girl who was so driven to get to Italia Conti, to be a model, then an independent girl about town, an actress. My life when I was 21 was a testament to my strength and now it had all fallen apart. I just couldn't understand how I'd lost it, all that confidence. How had I let it slip away? The damage done to me by the men I had loved seemed irreparable. What could fill the huge hole at the centre of my world?

I went to see another doctor, then another, and to each one I detailed my medical problems, my back, my lung, my head. I seemed to have a doctor for everything. I was describing my physical pain in the hope that it would somehow solve my mental problems. There was no choice. I had to work and look after the kids: these were the two things that kept me going. These and the new social life that I crafted for myself. I invited friends like Jess Morris, Fran Culter, Rose Ferguson and Kate over for dinner, and we would all join in on impromptu tap-dancing sessions and singalongs. I'd put on my tap shoes to escape my head, as I did when I was a child and sung songs like 'My Name Is Tallulah' from *Bugsy Malone*. We'd fill the house with laughter and song but for me it was tinged with desperation, as if the good time was staving off the abyss. These friends would always have to leave again and I'd still have to wake up alone. I was running on adrenalin and the panic attacks that I'd had all my life now became intense, manic even. Suddenly I was sensitive to every sound and couldn't stop myself from fidgeting when other people were sitting calmly and chatting. The house became a manifestation of my mind, with me putting everything away out of sight, in boxes. I cleaned and scrubbed every surface and couldn't abide the sight of a coat or a pair of shoes left abandoned on the floor. If one thing gave, then the whole house of cards in my fragile mind would come down. This was the devil of the manic illness: one minute I felt lucid, clear-headed and intensely happy. I would sit and write poetry, design clothes and create stories. The energy that I felt knew no bounds and this got me through the inevitable fall that would follow, down the plughole to hell. The only place I felt safe was in the darkness of my bedroom, wondering how just a few hours before I could feel so euphoric, knowing it was an illness yet still not able to ask for help. The panic attacks that had visited me all my life now came knocking almost every day and normal life stopped. I was crippled.

If I ever went out for the evening with the gang, we'd have a few drinks but then the real problems set in. One night I was travelling in a taxi and the others were chatting happily, but all I could see and feel were hundred of forks flying into my skin and leaving little puncture marks. I put my hand on the handle of the car door. I wanted to jump out, and had we not been going along at 60 miles per hour I probably would have. It was time to go back to the doctor, because by now I wasn't sleeping or eating properly. There seemed to be no way to induce sleep, so they sent me to a sleep clinic in a bid to solve the problem. First of all the doctors made me breathe into paper bags so that I was able to control my breathing and would not hyperventilate. I had to relearn the basic

COMING HOME

human functions of eating and sleeping. Then I was put into a dark room with all stimuli taken away. After a couple of days, sleep came, and when it did, it didn't leave me. I was sleeping up to 18 hours a day in the clinic and the doctors eventually sent me home with a directive to try to normalise my sleep patterns. But how could I when the fundamental problem was still there? My broken heart, what could normalise that?

On my birthday in June 2003 a group of us ended up in a Spanish restaurant in Soho and threw a party in an attempt to pretend to myself that I was OK, coping. Mairead and Tabitha, who together were the band Queens Of Noize, turned up with Carl Barât of the Libertines, who were getting a reputation for being *the* band of the zeitgeist. I got talking to Carl, who seemed like such a sensitive and interesting man, and that night we ended up writing poetry and drawing silly pictures of each other. He proved to be well-read and intelligent without being a snob about it. It was inspiring to meet a man who was so in touch with his emotions, but there was no romance, simply companionship. He told me not to give up on love and that it would prevail in the end. He was a temporary remedy for the pain and in that moment he gave me a flicker of hope. I wanted to believe he was right but knew it was pointless to hold a candle for the revival of my marriage. After that night my mood became low again and Kate came up with a solution. She called me to say that she and her mother, Linda, were taking Lila to a secluded hotel in Spain for a relaxing break and that I should join them.

'Snap out of it, Frostypants, it's time to pull yourself together and get a holiday,' she said.

My mother agreed it was a good idea, so I left the kids with her for a few days and headed off with Kate and Linda to Seville. The drive to the hotel got prettier by the minute, and then we pulled into a driveway surrounded by orange and olive trees. Through my dark glasses the house itself looked utterly beautiful, with its shuttered windows, sprawling outbuildings and vines tumbling down the walls of a spacious courtyard. We were met by Charlotte Scott, the proprietor, who introduced us to her son, George, the maître d' of the establishment. The Scotts were expats who had decamped to this paradise in Andalucia and the whole family was involved in running the place. After I was shown to my room, the shutters were closed and I slept. As the days rolled by I would hear shrieks of laughter and chatter from Kate and Lila, along with the other sounds of normal life going on. Kate would come and call me for breakfast and I'd go back to sleep, spending the first week in a semi-coma, hiding from the world.

There was a knock on my bedroom door and a tall figure shuffled in quietly, thinking I was asleep.

'Uh, here's your breakfast, tea and toast,' said the stranger, and I opened one eye and stared at him through the gloom. Who was he?

'Thanks,' I mumbled as he slipped out again.

COMING HOME

Occasionally I would get up and sit in the courtyard and the same man would bring me tea, silently and without fuss, as before. I barely noticed him, I was so caught up in my own pain. Sometimes I would see him glance at me curiously, this lady hiding behind dark glasses, staring into the distance. Meanwhile Kate was having an amazing time, playing music and singing while I would sit in my little iron chair stretched out like a cat, observing this slim, ethereal man darting about the hotel like a will-o'-the-wisp as he ran errands.

At the end of the first week Charlotte Scott gave a dinner party and I sat next to her. The man turned out to be her son, Jackson, and he sat opposite me. Charlotte was a lovely woman, sincere and frank, and she looked me in the eyes and read my pain. 'I have one piece of advice for you, Sadie,' she said seriously, twisting the stem of the wine glass in front of her. 'Stay clear of younger men.' I smiled at her and nodded, but at that very moment turned my eyes to Jackson, who raised his eyes to mine. We held each other's gaze and I felt I was looking at him for the first time, taking in his astonishing blue eyes, tanned skin and long, brown hair. His white shirt was open to his chest and revealed a smooth, bronzed chest adorned with beaded necklaces. Taken by an unstoppable force, I stretched my leg out under the table and touched his. He smiled and the attraction was instantaneous. I felt alive again, that there was something worth living for. I think that we fell in love in that instant.

The second week was spent getting to know each other. Jackson was gentle and kind and the perfect antidote to my relationships at home. He had been brought up in Andalucia and played flamenco guitar wonderfully, like a professional. He knew nothing about the laws of celebrity and had no idea who I was, or even who Kate was. This gave me hope that our relationship could be more than a holiday romance and I knew that his relaxed ways would calm me down. We would swim and walk through the groves of trees while he picked nuts and fruit and opened them with his teeth before giving them to me to taste. As we kissed, I thought about his mother's words to me a few days before at dinner. Here I was, kissing a younger man, a man in his mid-twenties, while I was in my mid-thirties. Yet I was incapable of resisting my basic human need for love and affection.

When Kate and I left at the end of the week, Charlotte came to see us off. I met her eyes gingerly and apologetically, as by this time she had guessed, by the way we looked at each other, that Jackson and I were smitten. Nevertheless she smiled and gave us her blessing, obviously knowing what a good man he was.

A week later Jackson arrived in England to stay with me and we fell deeper in love. I introduced him to the kids and they loved him because he was so natural and relaxed, always having time for them. But there was intense press interest in my new relationship and that was difficult for Jackson, who was trying to conduct a new

COMING HOME

relationship in the full glare of the tabloids. When it all got too much we would flee to Andalucia to his parents' hotel and hide from the world. I went to flamenco classes and let myself be absorbed into the pace of life in Seville, sleeping in the afternoon and partying at the Ferias (fairs) late into the night.

For the next two years I needed no therapy or medication to live my life. Jackson got me through it. Throughout this time, though, I had the divorce from Jude to negotiate and that was incredibly traumatic. Jackson and I had a lot to contend with but our relationship stayed strong and we took trips with the children to Costa Rica, America and India. After recovering from the postnatal depression I wanted to give the children even more love, especially focusing on Rudy, conscious all the time of the need to make it up to him. I would get all the children together in my bed, and I loved the tender moments that we shared. Rudy would be clutched to my breast, his blond curls running rampant on his head, Iris beside me singing gently and, lounging at the foot of my bed, Fin and Rafferty, telling me about their school work. Now it was just me and my gang and it was very liberating and gave me strength to go on as a single mother, and because that was who I was, I felt it made my relationship with them stronger. I knew that the media portrayed me as the victim in the break-up of my marriage, but I never ever wanted to be one, and so together me and my gang just kept going.

Soon I got offered a television series by BBC3. I wasn't in the right state of mind to take on such a big challenge but I needed some impetus to kick-start my career and this was it. It was to be called *What Sadie Did Next* and was based on the idea of me meeting and interviewing famous and inspirational people like Howard Marks, Michael Madsen, Carrie Fisher and Gwyneth Paltrow. As filming began I felt some of my old confidence return, but this was marred by a phone call I got one day in the middle of a shoot.

'Sadie? It's me, Sunny. It's about Dad. He's sick.'

'What do you mean? How sick?'

'Very,' replied Sunshine, waiting for my response, but I didn't know what to say. In the middle of my own meltdown, my relationship with my father was non-existent. He had estranged himself from all of his children, living hand to mouth in Ashton on the fringes of insanity. We'd all tried and failed to help him, and now, at a time when I really needed to focus on my own career for a while, here he was, rearing his ugly head, even if it was through illness. I didn't want any kind of emotional reunion with him, and so I chose not to believe it.

'He's done this before, Sunny,' I said. 'He's told us he's ill so one of us will take him in.'

'I think it's different this time,' Sunshine replied, before ending the call. I went back to the set and forgot about it, thinking it was another one of my dad's ploys. In the recent past he'd turned up on my doorstep and refused to leave and I'd had to call the police.

COMING HOME

When I got home from filming, a neighbour told me that my father had indeed been hanging around, sleeping in a van on the street outside the house, and that he'd been sick on the pavement. I was instantly filled with panic and dread. I couldn't deal with him, not now, not sick, and I pushed it from my mind again. A few days later I got a call from a nurse at a hospital in Ashton, who told me that my father had been admitted and was very ill, waiting for a liver transplant. If he didn't get one soon, he would die.

I put down the phone and sat silently for a long time. This was it. The time had come for me to confront my worst fears: life and death. I'd been in denial for a long time about the state of his health. Or perhaps I just didn't recognise serious illness. There had been no death or ill health in my family and my grandparents were living long and healthy lives.

Either way, now I couldn't run away any more. I packed a bag and went to Manchester, calling my half-brothers to tell them that I was on my way. When I got to the hospital I didn't recognise my dad. He smiled when he saw me, his head covered in a familiar tea cosy, but he was thin and gaunt. He looked more like a Tibetan monk than my bull-strong father. Simon, Jamie, Toby and Sunshine sat around his bed and I kissed him, but in reality it was hard to even look at him. When he slept one of us would stay with him while the others went for a cup of tea. My brothers told me about what I'd missed, about him living like a refugee in Mossley Road with no possessions apart from the house itself. I went back into the ward to say goodbye to Dad but found I couldn't do it, couldn't say what I wanted to say, so I said nothing. After that I went to finish filming for the BBC, interviewing Pete Docherty and Carl Barât together, the two frontmen of the Libertines. We three met on the banks of the Thames and did some busking, singing 'Don't Look Back Into The Sun'.

As we sang our hearts out the sun was setting over the river and I had a moment of intense sadness, because I was having fun and felt it was a shame that my father couldn't be there to enjoy the sort of spontaneous creativity that he was all about.

I went back to visit him twice more but each time leaving was the same, just as difficult. There was so much to say, where could I start? My brilliant father, who had loved me to distraction, was slipping away from me and all that seemed to remain was the hurt and the pain. I had to remind myself of how being so loved by him had made me feel, how special it had been and that no other man could come close to that devotion.

A few days later, in December 2003, I received a call to tell me that Dad had died. I descended to a new level of mourning, heartbroken all over again. At the funeral in Manchester I saw my two older half-brothers, Tim and Daniel, for the first time in 20 years and all the siblings sat together and talked about what a remarkable soul Dad had. Dad had asked that 'Hurt', by Johnny Cash, should be played at the funeral and that sent me desperately over the edge as I wept uncontrollably at the thought of the depression that had dogged him all his life.

After the funeral me and my five half-brothers and Sunshine all became very close again in a bid to keep Dad alive in some way. But just to look at Toby was enough as he was the spitting image of Vaughany.

Back in London I began to live as my father had, drinking red wine and staring at my reflection for a long time in the mirror, my wine-stained lips bleeding like my internal demons.

Now I really am alone, I really am alone in the pain that is my mind.

A dream. Or was it?

'Nine-nine-nine. Call an ambulance. I have warm blood pouring out of my mouth. I am dying,' I scream. Thick, hot liquid comes up like an elevator in my throat, making it hard for me to breathe. I am drowning in my own blood. 'Call 999. I don't know what's happening.'

In moments of panic and pure life and death there's no room for niceties.

'Call me the FUCKING DOCTOR NOW.' I'd learned early on that when there was a crisis, a doctor, a hospital, a friendly ambulance, could help me. As I slipped in and out of consciousness I heard the very familiar sound of an ambulance coming to get me: DAH-DAH DAH-DAH.

'Please just give me something for the pain, it hurts so bad,' I begged.

'Ahhh,' I say, grabbing my back. The nurse rushes over

and scrabbles for a vein. The big needle hovers over my arm like a mosquito waiting to go in for the kill. The nurse waits until she can get some stillness from my pain-shuddering body.

'OK, this is strong pain relief,' she says, jabbing it into my translucent arm.

'It will start to feel better ... now,' her voice lightly echoed as I was getting further and further away but in fact she was still close. As her voice disappeared so did the pain and I entered into a tunnel of relief where no physical or mental pain could affect or cause me harm. I floated along carried by the morphine they'd given me.

PRESENT DREAM: I am curled into a tight ball on my bed. So tight, so coiled. So I can stop any part of my body from flying off. I don't want my head to fall off. Or maybe that would be a good thing.

I can hear Zoe's breath as she sits and waits. 'What do you want me to do?' she gently nudges. I close my eyes tight to make sure I can close the world completely out. I don't know how long I have been lying there. Hours? Minutes? I have no idea.

'What do you want me to do?' she repeats.

My stomach feels like it has an ever-expanding breezeblock in it that is cemented to its fragile walls.

I can't eat, I can't sleep and now I feel I can't breathe.

'You can't go to your premiere, Sadie. You do realise that?' Zoe presses.

COMING HOME

'I know,' I say, beaten. 'Where can I go?'
'Hospital – I think you should go to hospital.'
DAH-DAH DAH-DAH. I hear the ambulance pull up and then voices outside get nearer. Inside the ambulance we sit in silence and I rock back and forth. It is as if I actually stopped I WOULD stop! The ambulance men speak to me to keep me distracted but I can't hear or see them. I am stuck, stuck in some painful psychosis that started a long time ago, as I retreat back into my hospital security blanket like a hermit crab into his hole. I can't carry a hospital on my back for ever.

Pain. Why does it follow me? I remember the first time when I was a rag doll of a child. Tightly fastened to a stretcher or heavily tucked into a trolley being pushed around the long, draughty corridors of UCH as my porter and nurse discussed the weather or what they were going to have for lunch. It seemed futile as all I could think about was, were they going to slice out my lung? I was so scared I wanted to make it better but I couldn't. Fear lived in every cell in my body, multiplying with each breath. Something make it better. THE DREAM IS OVER.

It was the end of the hot summer of 2005 and I split up with Jackson. Nothing caused it apart from the relationship having run its course. It meant I was alone again and life seemed impossible once more. There was no hope and nothing to look forward to and no man to define me. Mairead introduced me to Russell Brand at a party around the same time. We got talking and he told me about his battle with his own demons, clearly seeing something in me that was similar to his own struggles. Russell put me in touch with his counsellor, Chip, who ran a treatment centre, and soon I found the courage to give him a call. I'd been holding all this stuff in for so long that now it felt as if the years of childhood pain and all the times since then that I'd refused to deal with it were bursting to get out of me, leaking from my seams like a bulging bag of rubbish.

I met Chip on the street outside his treatment room and followed him up the path. He seemed like a kind and gentle guy, fishing in his bag to find the key to open the door. Inside I was shivering and praying for him to find that key and get the door open.

Please, please, please, just let me in…

The rubbish sack that was my body was splitting and the urge to talk was so great that I felt I couldn't wait any longer. Tears welled up as Chip found the key and then couldn't open the door.

'Sorry about this, Sadie,' he said, smiling. 'Bloody lock always sticks.'

Eventually the door opened and he went inside, and by the time I'd crossed the threshold the bag broke and unleashed a torrent of tears from inside me. Chip just listened as I let it all come out and didn't stop crying for an hour and a half. After that he made me tea and we came up with a plan for me to continue seeing him. I told him that I felt that part of my life was over, the part that contained

COMING HOME

alcohol and parties. I'd had enough of both and felt that booze had no further role to play in my life.

As I left I had an overwhelming feeling of light. Although still engulfed in darkness, I had a sense that something new had begun, something about finding out who I really was. I started to see Chip every week and began to come to terms with my past instead of getting drunk and crying about it. I was never reliant on alcohol or even used it every day; it was more that I couldn't handle it when I did drink – who it made me into. It meant that I couldn't *do* my life, my career and my children, and without it, I could keep everything in balance. I took up yoga and the gym and my sessions with Chip made things look much more manageable. Yet despite all this, I still felt that I could do it my way. I could still have the occasional night out and couple of glasses of wine and I didn't have the courage to give it up completely even though my life was suddenly becoming rosier now that Chip was in it.

I decided that I needed a friend to move in and she arrived in the shape of Mairead Nash, of Queens Of Noize, who had a big, Cheshire-cat smile and big, brown doe eyes and never failed to make me smile. The point of having her to stay with me at the house was her company, her energy and fun plus the fact she was sober too. It was 2007 and Mairead had just discovered a new singing sensation called Florence Welch. It seemed like another period of my life when I was back going to gigs and discovering new music. My house became a hive of activity, with Mairead bringing round a DJ friend of hers, Nick Grimshaw, a geeky but gorgeous boy from Oldham. I warmed to him instantly and we all became a new gang, fighting over the contents of my fridge. I also met a singer and actress from Manchester called Colette Cooper, who would come round and we would empty the hummus on to a plate and chop some vegetables while Grimmy would criticise us and Colette made endless cups of tea.

'Cup of tea? Cuppa tea? *Cup of tea!*' she'd shout.

'Bloody shut up about bloody tea, you bloody bleeder,' Grimmy would tell her.

Mairead would be curled up on the sofa with one of my two white Bichon Frisé pups.

'Why don't we have a party in the garden this weekend?' she suggested one day.

'Yeah, it can be the Pink Ladies. We'll all dress up.'

'No, it should be like a mini festival – Frostenbury,' suggested someone. That weekend we partied in the garden, with more food and music, but no booze. These people were my newfound family and Grimmy my surrogate son.

It was June 2008 and the summer was threatening to splutter into life, with an occasional hot day heralding a lazy few months ahead, none of which particularly excited me until one day I got sent a great script out of the blue, and curled up on my sofa to read it. The script, a one-woman show called *Touched For The Very First Time*, by playwright Zoe Lewis, absorbed me totally. I related to the

COMING HOME

story of a girl from Manchester who was unable to be happy with herself and was constantly striving to 'have it all'. I thought about my own life, my own fight to be a modern woman, and so the story resonated deep down inside me and I called my manager to tell him that I was interested. There was a flicker of fire in my brain and I realised that playing this role could change my fortunes and the direction of my life and would be a new focus to inspire me.

I woke on the day of the audition with a hangover. My plan to manage my own recovery wasn't exactly going according to plan and, being nervous, I'd gone out for a few drinks the previous evening. Nevertheless, I grabbed the script and made my way to the casting to read for the play's producer, Imogen Lloyd Webber, and the director, Douglas Rintoul. As soon as I sat down there was a pair of serious faces across the table telling me to start whenever I wanted. The whole thing was quite surreal as I felt as I had all my life, something of an impostor. When it was over, despite being polite, they didn't give me any indication that I'd impressed and so I assumed I hadn't got it and went home to sleep off the hangover. The next day Francis, my manager, called me to say that I'd been offered the part. I couldn't believe it and closed my eyes, thanking a God that I never talked to for giving me such a great opportunity. Rehearsals were due to start in the autumn so I had time to get myself completely together and focus, but before then I decided I would enjoy the summer.

In the morning I'd get up and go to Kundalini yoga and then to the gym. I'd take gong baths at the Alchemy Centre in Camden Town: a man came and banged a gong, which was supposed to enhance relaxation and connect you with your spirit. I made sure that the energy at my house was very Zen and that I was religious in my devotion to my inner health and happiness.

Then, one hot day in August, when the children were away, a sequence of events began to unfold. I'd been to yoga and was feeling revitalised when I decided to walk home via a restaurant where I knew a gang of friends would be hanging out. Well, what the hell, I thought, I deserve a glass of wine, so I went in and joined them. A full-on party ensued, then it was 'All back to mine!' The next morning I opened one eye and surveyed the nuclear fallout that was my house. It looked like World War III had hit it and I struggled to get into the shower, my head was so fuggy and dim. I knew that I'd way overdone it. What's more, that day I had to go to a children's party where the theme was fancy dress and there was nothing I felt like doing less. My demons were still there, laughing at me, pointing fingers.

See? You can't do it, can you? You can't banish us, we are too strong.

I arrived at the party to be greeted by a mêlée of friends all decked out in perfect fancy dress. Kate had come as a clown and my mother, who was now nannying for her, was also there. They took me inside and made me a cup of tea but they could see something was wrong. I had made minimal effort with my costume and felt like a fish out of water in this perfect summer scene of children running round the perfect English garden. Then there was me, feeling hungover and washed out. A friend gave me a lift home and, as I got into bed and closed my eyes, relief washed over me. It was over. I knew that was the last time, the last party, the last drink. Despite the knowledge that you can never say never, I knew that the next morning I would be a new Sadie.

As summer turned to autumn I dedicated myself to my new sober life and having counselling with Chip. Most of all, I had this huge part to learn for *Touched*, which was to start rehearsing towards the end of the year. The play was a 60-page script and the age range of the character was 14 to 37. As well as learning the script I had to look at all the other aspects of my life. FrostFrench had hit major problems because of the recession and our backer had pulled his money out. We went into administration but Jemima and I decided to give it another go and bought the company back. Now we had a fight on our hands. We streamlined the business and cut a lot of staff. There were parts of the design process that were too complicated, so we focused instead on the bits that had always done well, like the line of lingerie we designed for Debenhams. With Jemima and I back at the helm doing all the designing, we became more free to create what we wanted and got back some of the old fire. Even so, rescuing the business meant some brutal and emotional decisions which tested our relationship, but Jemima and I pulled together and got through. Sometimes when I looked at her across the table it was amazing to think how far we'd come since first setting eyes on each other at a warehouse party in Dalston aged 16.

Back at home, I would get up at five in the morning in order to do three hours of script learning before making the school run with the kids. I didn't have a nanny and nor did I want one, so I had to fit the memorising in when I had a spare moment. I made mood boards to set up my character's journey. I would use pictures, songs or poems as inspiration and she began to take on a life in me. I related to her chaotic childhood and hippy parents. More than that, I spent hours watching early videos of Madonna, the subject of the play, and was infected by her ability to reinvent, change and continually not give a damn what anyone else thought. Yes, she'd got a lot wrong in her past, but she always came back stronger.

When the rehearsals began on a chilly morning in December, it hit home what I'd let myself in for. It was a huge task, especially because I hadn't acted on stage for so many years. The director, Douglas, was a classically trained man from the more serious side of theatre and was precise and professional. For the next two months I was to be shut in a room with him and the production manager, the two of them putting me through my paces. The show was to open at Trafalgar Studios in the West End in

COMING HOME

February 2009, so there was pressure to get it to the required standard. Douglas was clever and also kind, and, like every time I encountered an intelligent, creative soul, I fell a little bit in love with him. The problem was that I had the constant feeling that he felt I wasn't up to it, but I knew this was my own neurosis and I couldn't let it take over my head. I had to trust this slightly scary man completely and soon I was so overloaded with information, what to feel, what to say, how to dance, where to stand, that I thought I was going slightly mad. Despite this, we broke the play down really well and in fact I realised that I was completely spoiled working one-to-one with such a skilled director. In all my acting career I'd never learned so much or been given so much attention. The nearer we got to the opening night, the more the fear grew. How could I stand up in front of 90 people every night on my own for well over an hour?

Douglas was such a perfectionist that he would bring up every tiny thing that I was doing wrong, and it made me want to cry. There were times when he would look at me with horror on his face, but I learned a lot about the power of the mind and trusted him as a director, so there weren't really any negative moments during the rehearsal period. Once we were into the dress rehearsal at the theatre, the nerves started. My dressing room was deep in the bowels of the Whitehall Theatre, which was a cavern of alleyways and smelled as if it was steeped in theatrical tradition. Here I was, starring in my own off-West End show, and I set about kitting out my dressing room with photographs of my father and my children and making it homely. Also on at the theatre was Joe Orton's *Entertaining Mr Sloane*, starring Matthew Horne and Imelda Staunton, and on the first night I got a note from Matthew wishing me good luck.

Walking out on to the stage to the strains of Madonna's 'Like A Virgin', I was greeted by a packed theatre of dimly lit faces. There was nowhere to run, here I was, I'd arrived, and over the next 80 minutes I'd sink or swim. Douglas and I had done a lot of work on the need for me to block out the audience, who were literally right on the stage, with blocks of seating bearing down on me on three sides. The set was simply a crumpled bed, like Tracey Emin's, surrounded by the detritus of years of womanhood. During the previews, once I was on stage my mind had started to play tricks on me and I'd imagined people in the audience that I knew and it would start to feed into my psyche and stop me acting. To combat this, I spent an hour before the press-night show cutting myself off from the world in the cocoon of my dressing room and took myself to a place where no one could reach me.

Then came the moment I couldn't put off any longer. It was the first night, the reviewers were in and I had to perform. Like waiting in the wings while doing *Mumbo Jumbo* 20 years previously, I felt as if I was watching myself from the outside and as I walked on stage I left my body and had to become Lesley, the character. At the end of the show I was stunned to receive a standing ovation. It began to sink in that I'd done well.

The next morning, after being told not to read the reviews by the producer, I was called and told that I'd come out of it pretty well and the reviewers had roundly applauded me for tackling such a mammoth role. I was able to relax a little and start to get into the role. Night after night I had my close friend Heidi to help me dress and change but the nerves didn't go and she would have to push me out on to the stage at the start of every performance. The next six weeks carried on in the same vein and all my family and friends came to see the show, including my brothers from Manchester, my mum and Holly, and then the gang: Kate, Rhys Ifans, Rose Ferguson and Carl Barât. Everyone had a complete laugh as the show bounced along, infused with music and nostalgia.

My home life was moving to a new level thanks to committing to sobriety and the clear-headedness it brought me. I would get up at five every morning and threw myself into exercise, adding trapeze and circus skills to my repertoire. It was a great excuse to catch up with plenty of old friends, most of whom I roped in to come and try trapeze with me, friends like Amanda Mealing from Italia Conti, who played Connie Fisher in *Holby City*, Ania Sowinski and Lisa Dwan. At last I faced my fear of heights as I swung on a trapeze 20 feet above the ground and flew through the air to be caught by a man on the other trapeze. Sometimes I took Iris along and we made it our special thing. Mairead moved out of the house and Jade, my sister, moved in. My therapy with Chip had also healed a lot of the issues, including some with my mother, who had by now had enough of the country and moved to London to be closer to her daughters.

After one of the last performances of *Touched* I got a letter from a casting director called Irene East, asking if I would be interested in doing some repertory theatre with a company called Love and Madness run by artistic director Neil Sheppeck. I was interested because *Touched* had been such a liberating and confidence-boosting experience, and so I went for a meeting. My fears were that this company was relatively small and unknown and what they were suggesting was for me to act in two of their plays in what would essentially be a fringe production.

On the plus side, they offered me a lot of creative input about the play that I was to star in, including casting. It appealed to me to get stuck in and do some good old-fashioned hard work. When I read the play, *Fool For Love*, it instantly resonated with me and I knew that I wanted to do it. As well as this play, I was to take a role in Shakespeare's *Richard III* with Carl Prekopp. Again I looked on this as a new opportunity to work with professional actors and learn more. But it was *Fool For Love* that excited me and I instantly knew who I wanted to play opposite me. I picked up the phone and called Carl Barât, who had told me that night we'd sat up late that he always wanted to act.

COMING HOME

'Are you still serious about acting?' I asked.

'Erm, yeah, I am,' he said with a nervous laugh.

'Well, go and buy a copy of *Fool For Love* and call me back if you like the part of Eddie.'

The next morning Carl called me back and left a message for me simply saying, 'I'm your Eddie.'

It was December 2009 and a year after starting rehearsals on *Touched* I was back at it with my two new plays. Again, I had to balance the work with looking after the children and preparing for Christmas. I made mood boards and had a dialect coach for the American accent for *Fool For Love*. It wasn't until we arrived at the rehearsal space that the company had found that I realised how different this experience was going to be from the one I'd had with *Touched*. For a start, we were rehearsing in Morden, south London, above a nail factory on an industrial estate. Once rehearsals started I knew that the level of direction I'd had for *Touched* wasn't going to be repeated on *Fool*, but all the same I needed to do *more, more, more*. I wanted the work because since giving up the booze I wanted to stuff my life full with creative projects. Even though everything was chaotic, and it was a struggle to even get to Morden through the snow and ice of the worst winter for 30 years, I was learning a lot about acting. I'd never been in a company before, and while we were rehearsing *Fool* in one room, we were also rehearsing *Richard III* in another. It was all about sharing coffee and cigarettes at break times and cheering up anyone who had a bad day. After some of the luxury I'd seen in my adult life, it was safe to say that I was back slumming it – and I loved it.

The plays opened at Riverside Studios in Hammersmith in February, and while *Fool For Love* received mixed reviews, *Richard III* had some impressive ones. And though the reviewers had taken a personal snipe at me and Carl, Carl took it on the chin and was even able to cheer me up. I became very fond of him and felt like I'd gained a little brother. I'll always remember the process of developing the whole production of *Fool For Love*. I realised it is not about the final performance but all the integral work that comes before it and I'd been acting with someone very special, that I loved and could identify with. My journey back to the stage seemed to bring me back in touch with my childlike love of performing and of fantasy, but also allowed me to be surrounded by people who work hard and hold up creativity as having ultimate importance in life, something that I too hold up as important, as did my father.

In my house today there is music and laughter with my children, as every weekend we amuse ourselves listening to Raff play the drums or Finlay singing some of the songs he has written or Iris practising the piano or Rudy playing the trumpet. The television is rarely on, as we don't need it. My gang of children are my closest friends and compatriots, growing up into creative people, and I look on in wonder as

COMING HOME

they take on their own personalities. Now I can even attend parents' evenings for my kids without being racked with the fear of authority that my father instilled in me. Until recently I wasn't able to see myself as an adult. Now, though, I see the ghost of my father receding into the distance, leaving me with happier memories of his artistry and sense of fun. There isn't a day that goes by that I don't think of him, or my beloved grandfather, who died recently, or my beautiful Grandma Betty, who is 90 this year and still going strong.

As I watch my house turn into something like the Von Trapps', I know that I can trust myself now and walk on solid foundations. I don't regret the past, nor do I dwell on it. I am just pleased that I can trust myself and others can too. Now that I can say that I've probably recovered from manic depression, or severe postnatal depression, which has weaved such a merry dance of destruction through my adult life, I've realised that, as a woman and a mother, depression is not something that we like to admit to. The stigma remains: as a mother you are supposed to cope and not admit defeat. I think I got some confusing medical advice for a long time and that didn't help, but ultimately what saved me was being able to ask for help and to accept it. It seems that admitting defeat was the best thing to do because as soon as I did, recovery was swift.

To come through and out the other end, into the light, you have to experience a lot of pain and this I did. As I stare at myself in the mirror and yank out the odd grey hair and study my wrinkles, I know there is no miracle to prevent the fact that I am getting older and now I gladly accept it. Yes, there are moments of loneliness that come with the territory but I now have a routine and rhythm to my life that I didn't have before. Every day I wake with my two dogs, four children and little sister Jade, 'my little gang'. We have at least seven cups of tea during the day and at night we have cups of cocoa and cuddles. Glamorous it ain't, but it's real life, and I'm happy. I put my head on the pillow and I as I close my eyes I say, 'Love you, Mum, love you, Dad. Night-night, sleep tight, don't let the bedbugs bite.'

Primrose Hill 2010

I wake – pick myself up – out of my bed – alone. My own two feet. Secure. Me. I walk. I flick the latch and jump the steps. I walk along on my own two feet. Left, right, left, right, along the paving. Along, along – past the fence – into the park. My breath is steady, my nose cold. I walk up and up, a path, a hill, dark green and dewy, into darkness.

I see buildings, lights, the birdcage, the Eye, the Gherkin. The change. I twist my head and look up. Stars, all the night's stars for me to see. Two new ones dance among them. Just for me.

Credits

Page 74 'Hold Me Close' written by David Essex ©1975 Stage Three Music (Catalogues) Limited, administered by Stage Three Music Publishing Limited. Lyrics used by permission

Page 152 lyrics from 'Gold' by Spandau Ballet reproduced by kind permission of Reformation Publishing Co Ltd.

Page 108 'Kooks' © 1971 David Bowie
Tintoretto Music/RZO Music Ltd/EMI Music Publishing Ltd (London W8 5SW)/Chrysalis Music Ltd

Printed in Great Britain
by Amazon